THE DIGNITY OF MAN
AS A PERSON

THE DIGNITY OF MAN
AS A PERSON

Essays on the Christian Humanism of
His Holiness John Paul II

Andrew Nicholas Woznicki, S.Ch.

WIPF & STOCK · Eugene, Oregon

Wipf and Stock Publishers
199 W 8th Ave, Suite 3
Eugene, OR 97401

The Dignity of Man as a Person
Essays on the Christian Humanism of His Holiness John Paul II
By Woznicki, Andrew Nicholas
Copyright©1987 Society of Christ in America
ISBN 13: 978-1-5326-5989-8
Publication date 6/5/2018
Previously published by Society of Christ, 1987

CONTENTS

Foreword
xi

Preface
xiii

I. The Biblical View of Man
1

II. On the Meaning of Marriage
29

III. On the Conception of
Catholic Education
47

IV. The Role of Christian Culture
69

V. The Catholic and the
Ecumenical Movement
89

VI. The Dignity of Being Human
113

VII. On Human Being as a Person
139

VIII. Humanistic Personalism
155

ACKNOWLEDGMENTS

Grateful acknowledgment is made to the following publishers for permission to quote and reprint from copyrighted material: Andrew N. Woznicki, "The Christian Humanism of Cardinal Karol Wojtyla," *The Human Person*, ed. by George McLean, Washington, 1979 © by the American Catholic Philosophical Association; Andrew N. Woznicki, *A Christian Humanism: Karol Wojtyla's Existential Personalism*, New Britain, 1980 © by Marie E. Lescoe; Andrew N. Woznicki, *Journey to the Unknown*, San Francisco, 1982 © by Golden Phoenix Press; Andrew N. Woznicki, "Ecumenical Consciousness According to Karol Wojtyla", *Center Journal*, 2, (1984), South Bent 1984 © by Center for Christian Studies; Andrew N. Woznicki, "The Christian Humanism and Adequate Personalism of Karol Wojtyla," *Pope John Paul II Lecture Series*, St.Paul, 1985 © by College of St. Thomas, St. John Seminary; Andrew N. Woznicki, "Revised Thomism: Existential Personalism Viewed from Phenomenological Perspectives," *Existential Personalism*, ed. by Daniel O. Dahlstrom, Washington 1986 © by the American Catholic Philosophical Association.

DEDICATION

To His Holiness
John Paul II
on the occasion
of his pilgrimage
to the
United States of America

September 1987

FOREWORD

Since assuming the Chair of Peter nine years ago, our Holy Father has courageously proclaimed the Gospel of Christ in every corner of the world. His historic visit to San Francisco affords us an occasion to celebrate our Catholic identity; more importantly, it is an opportunity for us to recommit ourselves to the values which the Pope has preached so effectively by word and deed: the dignity of the human person, the implications of the Gospel for individual and social morality, the relationship of dialogue between the Church and the modern world.

Pope John Paul is an energetic and prodigious teacher, and he has shared his vision of the Gospel in countless addresses, homilies and exhortations. In the series of essays contained in this volume, Father Andrew Woznicki explores several elements of our Holy Father's thought. His book provides a valuable resource, as it traces the development of the Pope's teaching from the years before his election, giving English language readers access to many writings previously inaccessible to them.

This book is a gift of Polish Catholics of the Bay Area, and its publication affords me an opportunity to thank them for the rich contribution they make to the life of the Church in San Francisco. I am grateful to Father Woznicki, Professor of Philosophy at the University of San Francisco, for sharing the fruits of his scholarship with us, and to the members of the Pastoral Mission of Saint Wojciech for their constant and devoted love for the Church, a love which they express with such zeal and generosity. I hope that many will find in The Dignity of Man as Person a path to a deeper understanding of the profound teaching of our Holy Father, Pope John Paul II.

John R. Quinn
Archbishop of San Francisco
June, 1987

PREFACE

In the history of the Catholic Church no Pope can compete with John Paul II in the sheer number of Apostolic visits to the followers of Christ living in *Diaspora* among different nations and races, various cultural and religious communities. St. John's "we believe in love" (I John 4:16) and St. Paul's "love of Christ urges us" (II Cor 5:14) compels John Paul II to make so many pilgrimages throughout the world in order to bring contemporary man closer to Our Lord Jesus Christ, who is the ultimate foundation in creating One Family of Man in God. In response to his spiritual concern for the well-being of–not only the faithful–but all men of good will, people have expressed their gratitude to Pope John Paul II in manifold ways: from a pig offered by Papuans during his visit to New Guinea, to statues and monuments constructed in other visited places.

I wish to express my deep gratitude more humbly in these few paragraphs, to Archbishop John Quinn, who typifies St. Paul's admonition "to preach the Word, be urgent in season and out of season, convince, rebuke, and exhort; be unfailing in patience and in teaching" (2 Tim 4:2). A special thanks goes to His Excellency for writing the Forward to this book.

The parishoners of the Polish Catholic Pastoral Mission of St. Wojciech in San Francisco, under the direction of their Pastor, Father Stanley Drzal, decided to commemorate the pastoral visit of the *Pontifex Maximus* to the City of the Golden Gate bridge, by making available in book form, John Paul II's thoughts related to the topics of his main spiritual concern. Consequently, following the inspiration of Polish writer and bibliographer, Jan Kowalik, the Parish Council of St.Wojciech Mission allotted special funds for the publication of this book in order to spread the basic teaching of the Pope and to share with their American friends.

The author of this book, with admiration and filial devotion, has attempted to sketch the Pope's basic and genuine message to contemporary man. With deep trepidation at delivering such an ambitious undertaking, the author hopes that he may, to some extent, contribute to a better understanding of the teaching of the present Deputy of Christ.

On this occasion, I would like also to express my thanks to numerous persons for their assistance in preparing this work. I wish to express my special gratitude to Mr. Jan Kowalik for his dedicated assistance in preparing the manuscript. He personally read and checked the entire text for accuracy. I am also greatly indebted to Rev. Wladyslaw Gowin, Provincial Superior of the American and Canadian Province of the Society of Christ, and Rev. Stanley Drzal, Pastor of the Polish Catholic Pastoral Mission of St. Wojciech in San Francisco, as well as to the parishoners, themselves, for their support in publishing this book.

• PREFACE •

It is no exaggeration to say that the publication of this book in such a timely manner would have been impossible without the assistance of Mr.Czeslaw Grycz. His diligent and artful skill in preparing this book for publication, while maintaining a genuine and contagious enthusiasm, not only gave us needed moral support, but is also greatly appreciated.

A.W.
San Francisco
September 1987

I. THE BIBLICAL VIEW OF MAN

In his search for the meaning of his existence, man has asked two questions namely, WHAT and WHO I AM.

By asking the question WHAT I AM, man followed the principle of intelligibility: understanding his nature. This question established his proximity and relationship to the surrounding reality and thus pointed to his destiny and purpose by finding his proper place in the universe. Time and space locations, as well as evolutionary directions, were of the utmost importance; for by knowing his nature man hoped to determine his own destiny.

After conquering the environment in which he exercised his nature, man began to ask himself the question WHO AM I? With this new question, the emphasis shifted from WHAT to WHO and consequently led to the discovery of a new identity. The question of identity, as the search for that with which man can identify himself, influences his understanding of the meaning and destiny of human existence. The contemporary crisis of man is, in fact, based on the ignorance and neglect of his "who-ness," his personal identifiable mark.

The shift from WHAT to WHO was necessitated by the fact that by concentrating exclusively on his "what-ness" man lost his sense of integrity as a human entity. Man is what he is not *already*, but he is what he is *not yet*. In the consciousness of contemporary man, the questions of WHAT and WHO have become ambiguous.

The question of WHAT I AM is therefore interdetermined with the question of WHO I AM. This mutual interdetermination can be formulated as follows: the more I know "what I am" the deeper I understand the answer to the question of "who I am" and *vice versa*.

The questions of WHAT and WHO I am originated when man started to wonder about himself. In the historical development of Western civilization, man's wonderment in regard to his own nature and existence was greatly influenced by the Bible.

I

The Bible describes man in a concrete way. But as time passed, this tradition has been stressed in different periods by different values and intellectual interests in what man is and who he is as a person. The philosophical and theological approaches of antiquity viewed man in a generic and abstract way. During the time of the Renaissance and thereafter, man was evaluated in his individuality and dignity. But since the advent of the industrial development, from the time of La Mettrie, man has been treated in a technological fashion, as *L'homme machine*.

Two accounts are given in the biblical description of creation. One is presented in the first chapter of *Genesis,* and the other is delineated in the following chapter of the same book. In the first is the story of the creation of the whole world, while in the second emphasis is given to the creative activity of God while bringing man into existence. Although these descriptions are not scientific presentations of the very beginning and cannot be treated as a cosmological account of the development of the universe, nevertheless in mythical form[1] they familiarize the reader with the image which primitive man had of himself. As such, these accounts represent the first revealed truth about the beginning of all of reality. Moreover, although the Bible gives several descriptions of man and his world, the first two chapters of *Genesis* have become a source of "inspiration for thinkers"[2] of all time.

To properly understand the biblical description of all reality, it is important that the reader be aware of the character of the texts of the first chapters of *Genesis.* Biblical criticism has pointed out that the first chapter is much younger than the second. It constitutes the so-called post-Exilic Elohist narration of divine creativity. The second chapter (with the third one which follows) belongs to the oldest biblical tradition. It is based on the Yahwist tradition which emphasizes the special intervention of God in the creation of man. The first chapter is called Elohist because in its narration God is named Elohim while the author of the second chapter used the Hebrew word Yahweh[3] for the name of God. Much more important, however, are the differences between these two descriptions of creation.

---

1   On the scientific and biblical approaches to the question on the origin of the world, see: A. Schøopfer, *Geschichte des Alten Testaments* (Innsruck: Verlagsanstalt Tyrolia, 1923), pp. 9-11; S. Stys, *Biblijny opis stworzenia wobec nauki* (Lublin: Towarzystwo Naukowe KUL, 1955).
2   "Biblical account of creation analyzed by Pope John Paul II, *L'Osservatore Romano,* September 17, 1979.
3   For the meaning of the words *Elohim* and *Yahweh,* see: *The New World Dictionary Concordance to the New American Bible* (New York: World Pub., 1970).

According to John Paul II, the Elohist narration gives a metaphysical description of man's original state. The Yahwist author(s) evaluates man in his axiological character and structure as a person. In the first narration we have an objective description, and in the second we have a subjective one.[4]

The first chapter of *Genesis* in the biblical narration on the creation of man gives a cosmological description of the creative activity of God. It also includes a sketchy image which depicts the origins of the human race. In this description, man is presented as the highest creature, one who is endowed with a special dignity.

As the highest being among all creatures, man is thus the ultimate result of God's creativity, the first in God's plan but the last to be created.[5] Along this same vein, Marian Filipiak, the biblical scholar, has written: "The basic idea of the first description of creation consists in revealing the primacy of man among all beings created by God."[6]

Man, as the highest being, was created by God only with His special assistance. In describing the creation of man in Gen. 1:27, the biblical author(s) uses the word *bah-rah* on three occasions. In the biblical sense, *bah-rah* does not mean a production of being from nothingness, but a process of prevailing over chaos, thereby changing it into cosmos: "creation signifies the victory over chaos."[7]

As a being specially created by God, man's origin stems from God himself. God does not create man by words alone, as in the case of other creatures. Only by God's special intervention was man created according to the image of God himself. In this respect, John Paul II comments:

---

4   "Biblical account", *L'Osservatore Romano*, cf. also Cardinal Karol Wojtyla, *Sign of Contradiction* (New York: The Seabury Press, 1979), pp. 19-26.
5   M. Filipiak, *Biblia a Człowiek* (Lublin, Towarzystwo Naukowe KUL, 1979), p. 72.
6   M. Filipiak, *Biblia*, p. 73.
7   *Ibid.* On the meaning of *bah-rah* 'salvation', see: A. Klawek, "Piesn o stworzeniu", *Ruch Biblijny i Liturgiczny*, 15 (1962), p. 153.

> Even though man is strictly bound to the visible world, nevertheless the biblical narrator does not speak of his likeness to the rest of creatures...but only to God....Man (however) is not created according to a natural succession, but the Creator seems to halt before calling him to existence, as if he were pondering within Himself to make a decision.[8]

This means that man was created according to the image of God himself: "Let us make man in our image after our likeness" (Gen. 1:26).

Having a likeness to God Himself, thus man is presented as a God-like being in his nature as a whole: "God created man (*ah-dahm* - a collective noun: humanity) in His own image; in the image of God He created him, male (*zah-chahr* - masculine) and female (*n'keh-vah* - feminine) He created them" (Gen. 1:27).[9]

To summarize, we have seen that the first account of creation by the Yahwist narration is a "cosmological" description of the world. As such, it is not oriented toward meaning-content, but instead stresses the meaning-value of the creative activity of God, giving a metaphysical insight into the very beginnings of reality. Accordingly, John Paul II says:

> The first account of man's creation which as we observed, is of a theological nature, conceals within itself a powerful metaphysical content. Let it not be forgotten that this very text of the Book of Genesis has become the source of the most profound inspirations for thinkers who have sought to understand "being" and "existence". (Perhaps only the third chapter of Exodus can bear comparison with this text.) Notwithstanding certain detailed and plastic expressions of the passage, man is defined there, first of all, in the dimensions of being and of existence *(esse)*. He is defined in a way that is more metaphysical than physical.[10]

---

8   "Biblical account", *L'Osservatore Romano*, cf. Cardinal Karol Wojtyla, *U podstaw odnowy* (Krakow: Polskie Towarzystwo Teologiczne, 1972), p. 39ff.
9   Cf. C. Jakubiec, *Pradzieje biblijne, Teologia Genesis 1-11* (Poznan: Ksiegarnia Sw. Wojciecha, 1968), p.25.
10 "Biblical account", *L'Osservatore Romano*. On the "inspiration" of Genesis, see: E. Gilson, *Le Thomisme* (Paris: J. Vrin, 1944) pp. 122-124.

The first description of creation refers to creation of the universe which is portrayed only as the place in which man is located. The second, however, is dedicated to man. "Adam" is, first of all, described as somebody who is taken from the earth. This is evident when the word is taken in its original context.

Here we can note a certain play on words, particularly in the terms of *ah-dahm* (man) and *adah-mah'* (earth), with the root of each found in *'dm*, which means "to be red." Redness expresses the similarity between the color of man's skin and the color of the earth.[11] The biblical message can therefore be interpreted by the following threefold correlation between man and earth: (1) man comes from earth (Gen. 2:7; cf. 3:19, 23), (2) it is man's duty to cultivate the soil (3:23), and (3) man will return to the earth after his death (3:19).[12] In contrast to the description of Adam-man in *Genesis* 1, the Adam-man of *Genesis* 2 is characterized as being specifically different from all the other creatures in that God gave significant meaning to human sexuality. In the narration of *Genesis* 2, the sexual differentiation made between male and female is rather obscure due to certain linguistic expressions such as the following: "Adam's sleep" (in Hebrew *tar-deh-mah'*) cannot be understood as a simple unconsciousness or a state of dreaming, since dreaming is defined in the Bible as *ghalohm* (cf. Gen. 15:12; 1 Sam. 26:12).[13] Commenting on the Hebrew expression *tar-deh-mah'* John Paul II says:

> If, by analogy with sleep, we can speak here also of a dream, we must say that the biblical archetype allows us to admit as the content of that dream a "second self," which is also personal and

---

11 Cf. C. Westermann, "Adam, Mensch", *Theologisches Wörterbuch zum Alten Testament* I (Stuttgart: Kohlhammer, 1973), pp. 41-57.
12 M. Filipiak, *Biblia*, p. 77.
13 Referring to Z. Freud, John Paul II observes: "Freud examines..., the content of <u>dreams</u> (Latin: *somnium*), which, being formed with physical elements 'pushed back into the subconscious' make it possible, in his opinion, to allow the unconscious contents to emerge; the latter, he claims, are in the last analysis always sexual. This idea is, of course, quite alien to the biblical author...', "Original unity of man and woman", November 12, 1979.

equally referred to the situation of original solitude, that is to the whole of that process of the stabilization of human identity in relation to living beings *(animalia)* as a whole, since it is the process of man's "differentiation" from this environment.[14]

"**Adam's helper**" (in Hebrew $^n geh'$-*zer*. Quoting translations of this passage into several languages, John Paul II writes:

> Since the term *aiuto* (help) seems to suggest the concept of "complementarity" or better of "exact correspondence", the term *simile* is connected rather with that of "similarity," but in a different sense from man's likeness to God.[15]

"**Adam's rib.**" The biblical expression for "rib" is *tzeh'-la^{n}g* and is identified by some scholars as "life."[16] Following this interpretation, John Paul II comments:

> It is interesting to note that for the ancient Summerians the cuneiform sign to indicate the noun "rib" coincided with the one used to indicate the word "life." As for the Yahwist narrative, according to a certain interpretation of Gen. 2:21, God rather covers the rib with flesh (instead of closing up its place with flesh) and in this way "makes" the woman, who comes from the "flesh and bones" of the first man (male).[17]

If the biblical expression *zeh'-la^{n}g* (rib) can be translated as life, then it can be easily understood how *chawwa* is the given name for Eve. In Gen. 3:20 there occurs another specific play on the words in which mean "living," is connected with "mother". *(ehm)* "mother of all living."

"**Adam-man**" as *eesh-eeshah* In the second chapter of *Genesis* another play on words concerning adam-man as *eesh-eeshah* is found. This contraposition stresses the sexual differentiation between man as male and female. The specific *genre litteraire* of Gen. 2, which is not comparable to any other known language in the world (J.M. Voste), has led some biblical

---

14 *Ibid.*
15 *Ibid.* Cf. Karol Wojtyla, "Instynkt, milosc, malzenstwo", *Tygodnik Powszechny*, 42 (1952).
16 Cf. J. Feldmann, *Paradies und Sündenfall* (Münster: Aschendorffsche Verlagsbuchhandlung, 1913), p. 241.
17 "Original unity," *L'Osservatore Romano*.

scholars to conclude that the twofold description of human sexuality as found in the first two chapters of *Genesis* is not contradictory. Instead, they are complementary. In other words, human sexuality should be understood in a positive sense, meaning that both sexes are equal in nature and that their differences are only functional. On this topic John Paul II writes:

> Corporality and sexuality are not completely identified. Although the human body, in its normal constitution, bears within it the signs of sex and is, by its nature, male or female, the fact, however, that man is a "body" belongs to the structure of the personal subject more deeply than the fact that he is in his somatic constitution also male or female.[18]

Although sexually differentiated into male and female, man nevertheless remains ontologically united by having the same nature. This ontic unity between man and woman becomes the foundation for marriage:

> Then, the Lord God said, "It is not good that the man is alone; I will make him a helper like himself..." And the rib which the Lord took from man, he made into a woman, and brought her to him. Then the man said, "She is now bone of my bone, and flesh of my flesh. She shall be called woman for from man she has been taken." For this reason a man leaves his father and mother and clings to his wife, and the two become one flesh (Gen. 2:18, 22-24).

The above text raises several questions which are biblical in form and philosophical in nature.

II

The main reason for the differentiation of Adam-man into male and female is due to the fact that the primordial human being experienced being alone. John Paul II remarks: "His body, through which man participates in the visible created world,

---

18 *Ibid.* Cf. Karol Wojtyla, "Zagadnienie katolickiej etyki seksualnej", *Roczniki Filozoficzne*, 2 (1965), pp. 5- 25.

makes him at the same time conscious of being alone."[19] But being alone also makes man a free being:

> In the concept of original solitude are included both self-consciousness and self-determination. The fact that man is "alone" conceals within it this ontological structure and is at the same time an indication of true comprehension.[20]

This "existential" explanation of the sexual differentiation between man as male and female[21] indicates that human beings are separated from other created beings and their nature receives new dimensions through which man is a person: "The analysis of the Yahwist text also enables us to <u>link man's original solitude with consciousness of the body,</u> through which man is distinguished from all the *animalia* and is 'separated' from them, and also <u>through</u> which he is <u>a person.</u>"[22] In other words, male and female constitute two different "dimensions of human being"[23] and show "the creation of man especially in its subjective aspect."[24]

If "Adam-man" is found to be sexually differentiated as "male-female," and if this sexual polarization of the opposite sexes shows each to be a person, then the unity between man and woman is by necessity a personal one. John Paul II reasons:

> Following the narrative of the Book of Genesis, we have seen that the "definitive" creation of man consists in the creation of the unity of two beings. Their <u>unity denotes</u> above all <u>the identity of human nature; the duality, on the other hand, manifests what, on the basis of this identity, constitutes the masculinity and femininity of</u> created man. This ontological dimension of unity and duality has, at the same time, an axiological meaning. From the text of Genesis 2:23 and from the whole context it is clearly

---

19 "Man's awareness of being a person", *L'Osservatore Romano*, October 29, 1979.
20 *Ibid.*
21 Cf. C. Jakubiec, "Adam i Ewa", *Ateneum Kaplanskie*, 52 (1950), pp. 115-
22 "Man's awareness", *L'Osservatore Romano*. Cf. Karol Wojtyla, "Czlowiek jest osoba", *Tygodnik Powszechny*, 52 (1964).
23 John Paul II, "Boundry between original innocence and redemption", *L'Osservatore Romano*, October 1, 1979.
24 *Ibid.*, "The second account of creation: the subjective definition of man", *L'Osservatore Romano*, September 24, 1979.

seen that man was created as a particular value before God ("God saw everything that he had made, and behold, it was very good": Gen. 1:31), but also as a particular value for man himself: first because he is "man"; second, because the "woman" is for the man, and vice versa the "man" is for the "woman." - While the first chapter of *Genesis* expresses this value in a purely theological form (and indirectly a metaphysical one), the second chapter, on the other hand, <u>reveals, so to speak, the first circle of the experience lived by man as value.</u>[25]

The unity and duality of "Adam-man" as a male and female constitute a specific communion between man and woman which should be understood as a relation between two persons. The ontological and axiological basis for the unity of man and woman in terms of a communion of persons is the foundation of human solitude:

> In this way the meaning of man's original unity, through masculinity and femininity, is expressed as an overcoming of the frontier of solitude, and at the same time as an affirmation - with regard to both human beings - of everything that constitutes 'man' in solitude.[26]

The personalistic unity between man and woman understood as a communion between persons requires mutuality. The reason for this is the consciousness of having the same body which, ontologically speaking, belongs to the same nature: "In fact, it bears within it a particular consciousness of the meaning of that body in the mutual self-giving of the persons."[27] Man's mutual self-giving consists "in the complementarity of what is male

---

25 "By the communion of persons man becomes the image of God," *L'Osservatore Romano*, November 19, 1979. Cf. Karol Wojtyla, "Religijne przezywanie czystosci", *Tygodnik Powszechny*, 6 (1953).
26 "By the communion", *L'Osservatore Romano*. Cf. Karol Wojtyla, "Rodzina jako 'communio personarum'. Proba interpretacji teologicznej", *Ateneum Kaplanskie*, 3 (1974), pp. 347-361.
27 John Paul II, "Marriage one and indissoluble", *L'Osservatore Romano*, November 26, 1979. Cf. idem, "The 'heart' a battlefield between love and lust", *L'Osservatore Romano*, July 28, 1980; "Adultery: a breakdown of the personal covenant", *L'Osservatore Romano*, September 1, 1980.

and female in him."[28] Mutuality, conceived in terms of complementarity remains, however, the characteristic of a gift. By exchanging their own persons man and woman are enabled not only to share their nature but also to enrich each other: "...the exchange of the gift, in which the whole of their humanity, body and soul, femininity and masculinity, participates, is actualized by preserving the interior characteristics (...) of the donation of oneself to the other as a gift."[29] Mutuality, then, enables man to find himself in the other as the other:

> ...this <u>finding of oneself in giving oneself becomes the source of a new giving of oneself,</u> which grows by virtue of the interior disposition to the exchange of the gift and the extent to which it meets with the same and even deeper acceptance and welcome, as the fruit of a more and more intense awareness of the gift itself.[30]

Conceived as an exchange of one's own person with another, mutuality reveals man in his truth.[31]

"Adam-man," understood as a being placed in the created world and conceived as a person made according to the image of God Himself, is both an <u>immanent</u> and a <u>transcendent</u> creature. Seen as an immanent being, the man of *Genesis* is revealed as an incarnated, praxeological and historical being. But the transcendentality of the human individual points to his spiritual life, divine destiny and conscience.

---

28 *Idem*, "Man and woman: a mutual gift for each other", *L'Osservatore Romano*, February 11, 1980. Cf. Karol Wojtyla, *Milosc i odpowiedzialnosc* (Kraków, *Znak*, 1962), pp. 73-77.
29 "Man and woman", *L'Osservatore Romano*. Cf. *Idem*, "Interpreting the concept of concupiscence", *L'Osservatore Romano*, October 13, 1980.
30 "Man and woman", *L'Osservatore Romano*.
31 *Ibid*. Cf. also Fr. Sawicki, Filozofia milosci (Kraków: Ksiegarnia Krakowska, 1945).

III

The biblical narration presents human reality not *in abstracto* but *in concreto*. According to the Bible, the most concrete datum of human reality is the body (*bah-sahr*) through which man can reveal himself as an existing being in the world: "...man is defined there (sc. in *Genesis*), first of all, in the dimensions of being and of existence (*'esse'*). He is defined in a way that is more metaphysical than physical."[32] As "self-revealing-being-in-the-world"[33] man, however, finds himself among other created beings.[34]

Accordingly, man becomes aware that by having a body he is, in a specific way, obliged to "till the earth" and "subdue it"; but as a person his "body is such as to permit him to be the author of truly human activity."[35]

The fact that by having a body man manifests himself as a person through his activity, and the fact that being sexually divided into masculinity and femininity, indicates that his incarnation is twofold. Referring to Gen. 2:23, John Paul II says:

> In the light of this text we understand that knowledge of man passes through masculinity and femininity, which are, as it were, two "incarnations" of the same metaphysical solitude, before God and the world - <u>two ways, as it were, of being a body and at the same time a man, which complete each other</u> - two complementary dimensions, as it were, of self-consciousness and self-determination and, at the same time, <u>two complementary ways of being conscious of meaning of the body</u>.[36]

In a word: "The body as the expression of person, was the first sign of man's presence in the visible world. In that world, man was able, right from the beginning, to distinguish himself,

---

32 John Paul II, "Biblical account", *L'Osservatore Romano*.
33 *Ibid*. "By the communion", *L'Osservatore Romano*.
34 John Paul II, "Man's awareness", *L'Osservatore Romano*.
35 "In the very definition of man is the alternative between death and immortality", *L'Osservatore Romano*, November 5, 1979.
36 "Marriage one", *L'Osservatore Romano*. Cf. Karol Wojtyla, "Mysli o malzenstwie", *Znak*, 7 (1957), pp. 595-604.

almost to be individualized - that is, confirm himself as a person - also through his body."[37]

There are two dimensions to the body of each individual man, i.e., the objective and subjective. In the former, human body constitutes "man object-thing," while in the latter human body constitutes "subject-person."[38] This twofold dimension of human body is the foundation for establishing various relationships between man and woman.

Generally speaking, the relationship between man and woman can take either a form of mutual belonging to each other as persons or it can take the form of a mutual appropriation of each other as things. This twofold relationship between man and woman is thus based on two different kinds of human intentionality: the first constitutes a communion of persons and "is carried out in the 'heart'...and the will";[39] while the second kind of intentionality becomes "a 'ground' of appropriation of the other person."[40] In other words, the mutual relationship between man and woman can be built upon either unilateral or bilateral attitudes towards each other's body, which means to treat the body of the other either as an object only or as a subject.[41]

The double dimension of the human body as an object and as a subject based on "the dimension of the intentionality of man's very existence"[42] results in a specific dialectical tension between man and woman which has either creative or

---

[37] "Real significance of original nakedness", *L'Osservatore Romano*, May 19, 1980.
[38] John Paul II, "Opposition in the human heart between the spirit and the body", *L'Osservatore Romano*, August 4, 1980.
[39] "Depersonalizing effect of concupiscence", *L'Osservatore Romano*, September 29, 1980. Cf. Karol Wojtyla, "Nauka encykliki 'Humanae vitae' o milosci", *Analecta Cracoviensia*, 1 (1969), pp. 341-356.
[40] "Opposition in the human heart", *L'Osservatore Romano*.
[41] Cf. "Redemptor Hominis", *Acta Apostolicae Sedis* 7 (1979).
[42] John Paul II, "Depersonalizing", *L'Osservatore Romano*. Cf. Karol Wojtyla, "Osoba i wspolnota", *Roczniki Filozoficzne*, 2 (1976), pp. 5-39; "The intentional and the human act that is, act and experience", *Analecta Husserliana*, 5 (1976), pp. 269-280.

destructive results. The destructive resolution of the dialectical tension between the intentionality of body as an object and body as a subject results as "the subjectivity of the person gives way, in a certain sense, to the objectivity of the body."[43] Such "intentional reduction...sweeps the will along into its narrow horizon, when it brings for the decision of a relationship with another human being (...) according to the specific scale of values of 'lust,' only then can it be said that 'desire' has also gained possession of the 'heart'."[44] The consequence of such an intentional reduction of another's body into pure objectivity is not only the fact that "the personal relationship becomes almost incapable of accepting the mutual gift of the person,"[45] but it also means that one loses the freedom over one's own body: "we can also speak of that more or less complete 'compulsion,' which is elsewhere called 'compulsion of the body' and which brings with it loss of the 'freedom of the gift,' congenital in deep awareness of the matrimonial meaning of the body."[46]

If the process of depersonalization in the relationship between man and woman takes place in the order of intentionality, then this same "dimension of the intentionality of man's existence" can also be a creative force in regaining "a full subjective dimension,"[47] which thus establishes a proper balance of human body both from within and from without. In the words of John Paul II: "...that it is the basis of the will, and the possibility of choosing and deciding, through which - by virtue of self-decision and self-determination - the very way of existing with regard to another person is established."[48] In other words, to establish the proper balance between body as an object and body as a subject, both man and woman must strive together for "the fundamental meaning characteristic of the perennial and reciprocal attraction of masculinity and

---

43 "The 'heart' a battlefield", *L'Osservatore Romano*.
44 "Depersonalizing", *L'Osservatore Romano*.
45 "The 'heart' a battlefield", *L'Osservatore Romano*.
46 "Depersonalizing", *L'Osservatore Romano*.
47 Ibid.
48 Ibid.

femininity, contained in the very reality of the constitution of man as a person, body and sex together."⁴⁹

The intentional dimension of human body is both ontological in nature and praxeological in character. Referring to the words of Christ (Matt. 19:5-6) John Paul II says: "...by warning against the lust of the flesh, he expresses the same truth about the ontological dimension of the body and confirms its ethical meaning, consistent with his teaching as a whole."⁵⁰

The ontological dimension of the body points to the priority of human subjectivity which constitutes the dignity of man as a person: "...the body as an element which, together with the spirit, determines man's ontological subjectivity and shares in his dignity as a person."⁵¹ However, this ontological subjectivity of human being is also the foundation for the "ethos of human practice" by man:

> Precisely in this sphere an <u>interpenetration of *ethos* and *praxis*</u> is carried out. Here there live their own life (not exclusively "theoretical") the individual principles that is, the norms of morality with their motivations, worked out and made known by moralists, but also the ones worked out - certainly not without a link with the works of moralists and scientists - by individual man, as authors and direct subjects of real morality, as co-authors of its history, on which there depends also the level of morality itself, its

---

49 *Ibid.* On the priority of person in the human relationship, see: Karol Wojtya, *Ocena mozliwosci zbudowania etyki chrzescijanskiej przy zalozeniach systemu Maksa Schelera* (Lublin: Towarzystwo Naukowe KUL, 1959); "Personalizm tomistyczny", *Znak*, 5 (1961), pp. 664-675; "O godnosci osoby ludzkiej", *Notificationes e Curia Metropolitana*, 12 (1964), pp. 287-289; "Czlowiek jest osoba", *Tygodnik Powszechny*, 52 (1964).

50 "Realization of the value of the body according to the plan of the Creator, *L'Osservatore Romano*, October 27, 1980. Person as a subject matter of ethics, Karol Wojtyla, "Natura ludzka jako podstawa formacji etycznej", *Znak*, 11 (1959), pp. 693-697; "Etyka a teologia moralna", *Znak*, 9 pp. 1077-1082.

51 "Realization", *L'Osservatore Romano*. Cf. Karol Wojtyla, "Tajemnice i czlowiek", *Tygodnik Powszechny* 11 (1957); "The Structure of Self-Determination as the Core of the Theory of the Person", in: *Congresso Internazionale Tomasso D'Aquino nel suo Settimo Centenario* (Rome/Naples, 1974), pp. 37-44; "Teoria e prassi nella filosofia della persona umana", *Sapienza*, 4 (1976), pp. 377-384; "Subjectivity and the Irreducible in Man", *Analecta Husserliana*, 7 (1978), pp. 107-114.

progress or its decadence.⁵²

The ontological aspect of human subjectivity is the basis for the mutual interexchange between man and woman of their masculinity and femininity which is "a part of all the rich storehouse of values with which the female appears to the man,"⁵³ and *vice versa*. In other words: "The eternal attraction of man towards femininity (cf. Gen. 2:23) frees in him - or perhaps it should free - a gamut of spiritual-corporeal desires of an especially personal and 'sharing' nature (...) to which a proportionate pyramid of values corresponds."⁵⁴ Therefore, the ontological dimension of human body consists of discovering the proper order of mutual self-giving of their persons; and by man and woman finding "the sphere of *'praxis,'* that is, in our behaviour and also in the concrete expression of values."⁵⁵

Mutual self-giving of their persons is the basis for "man's participation in exterior perception of the world," and the way to "the happy discovery of one's own humanity 'with the help' of the other human being."⁵⁶ This means that man does not remain on the external surface of the perception of the created world, but is able to participate in the world from within:

> In this way, the human body acquires a completely new meaning, which cannot be placed on the plane of the remaining "external" perception of the world. It expresses, in fact, the person in his ontological and existential concreteness, which is something more

---

52 "Gospel values and duties of the human heart", *L'Osservatore Romano*, October 20, 1980. Cf. Karol Wojtyla, "Il problema del constituirsi della cultura attraverso la 'Praxis' umana", *Rivisia di Filosofia Neoscolastica*, 3 (1977), pp. 513-524.

53 John Paul II, "Mutual attraction differs from lust", *L'Osservatore Romano*, September 22, 1980.

54 *Ibid.*

55 "Spontaneity: the mature result of conscience", *L'Osservatore Romano*, November 17, 1980. Cf. Karol Wojtyla, "Wychowanie milosci", *Tygodnik Powszechny*, 21 (1960); "Problem 'uswiadomienia' z punktu widzenia teologii," *Ateneum Kaplanskie*, 54 (1962), pp. 1-5; "O znaczeniu milosci oblubienczej", *Roczniki Filozoficne*, 2 (1974), pp. 151-174.

56 John Paul II, "Fulness of interpersonal communication", *L'Osservatore Romano*, December 24, 1979.

than the "individual," and therefore expresses the personal human "self," which derives its exterior perception from within.[57]

Being able to perceive reality from within and through other person(s), man can create new meaning and value for his existence through "interpersonal communication":

> In its original, and deeper meaning "communication" was and is directly connected with subjects, who "communicate" precisely on the basis of the "common union" that exists between them, both to reach and to express a reality that is peculiar and pertinent only to the sphere of person-subjects.[58]

This interpersonal communication has an "ontological dimension" which "<u>reveals, so to speak, the first circle of the experience lived by man as value.</u>"[59] Consequently, man in his unity and duality receives "an axiological meaning"[60] which should be realized in *praxis*.[61]

The first chapters of *Genesis* mention two states of the origin of man, namely, the state of original innocence, and secondly, the state of original fall. In John Paul II's view, these two states represent two dimensions of human being: (1) one which constitutes the pre-historical state, and (2) one which constitutes the historical dimension of human being.[62] Although both of these original stages of development are based on the human experience of man's corporality, the state of innocence was the result of God's creativity; but the original state of fall was caused by man's refusal to cultivate the divine image offered to him by choosing to follow his own image:

> Man's experience of his body, as we discover it in the biblical text quoted, is certainly on the threshold of the whole subsequent "historical" experience. It also seems to rest, however, at such an

---

[57] *Ibid.*
[58] "Fulness", *L'Osservatore Romano.*
[59] "By the communion", *L'Osservatore Romano.*
[60] *Ibid.*
[61] Cf. A. N. Woznicki, *A Christian Humanism: Karol Wojtyla's Existential Personalism* (New Britain: Mariel Publications, 1980), pp. 43ff.
[62] "Boundry", *L'Osservatore Romano.*

ontological depth that man does not perceive it in his own everyday life, even if at the same time, and in a certain way, he presupposes it and postulates it as part of the process of formation of his own image.[63]

As a result of the temptation to form one's own image, man lost his original state of innocence and initiated his alienation from the image of God, thereby losing the purity of his "heart."[64] In this process of alienation, however, man does not completely destroy the image of God in himself, but merely diminishes it:

> In fact, in the whole perspective of his own "history," man will not fail to confer a nuptial meaning on his own body. Even if this meaning undergoes and will undergo many distortions, it will always remain the deepest level, which demands to be revealed in all its simplicity and purity, and to be shown in its whole truth, as a sign of the "image of God." The way that goes from the mystery of creation to the "redemption of the body" (cf. Rom. 8), also passes here.[65]

The Bible describes this process of diminishing the divine image in man in various forms:

> Man loses, in a way, the original certainty of the "image of God," expressed in his body. He also loses to some extent the sense of his right to participate in the perception of the world, which he enjoyed in the mystery of creation. This right had its foundation in man's inner self, in the fact that he himself participated in the divine vision of the world and of his humanity; which gave him peace and joy in living the truth and value of his own body, in all its simplicity, transmitted to him by the Creator: "God saw (that) it was very good" (Gen. 1:31).[66]

---

[63] "Meaning of original human experiences", *L'Osservatore Romano*, December 17, 1979.

[64] Cf. John Paul II, "Creation: God's gift of Love", *L'Osservatore Romano*, December 21, 1978.

[65] John Paul II, "The man-person becomes a gift in the freedom of love", *L'Osservatore Romano*, January 21, 1980.

[66] *Idem.*, "Real significance of original nakedness", *L'Osservatore Romano*, May 19, 1980.

As a result of losing "the original certainty of the image of God," man experiences a disorder in his nature. The Bible describes this disorder in terms of shame:

> It is the shame produced in humanity itself, caused by the deep disorder in that on account of which man, in the mystery of creation, was "God's image," both in his personal *ego* and in the interpersonal relationship, through the original communion of persons, constituted by the man and the woman together.[67]

Feeling shame for his body leads man "to create a fundamental disquiet in the whole of human existence, not only in the fact of the prospect of death, but also before that on which there depends the value and dignity themselves of the person in his ethical significance."[68] This fear causes "the structure of self-mastery, essential for the person, is, in a way, shaken to the very foundations in him, he again identifies himself with it in that he is continually ready to win it."[69]

Describing the loss of the original state of innocence in terms of shame has a twofold meaning: "it indicates the true threat to the value and at the same time preserves this value interiorly."[70] As a result of this twofold loss, man becomes conscious of his existential ambiguity. This ambiguous character of being human consists of man's mode of existing in the world: existence appears both as a gift and as a betrayal; it is the foundation for both hope and despair; promise and threat; man wants to live yet he is certain of his death; he tends to be but he always turns into not to be; man searches for being but often finds experiences of absurdity ...in the words of the Bible, the ambiguous character of human existence is expressed in terms of a distortion of the original unity between man and woman: "The previous analysis of Genesis 3:7 already showed that in the new situation, after the breaking of the

---

[67] *Idem*, "A fundamental disquiet in all human existence", *L'Osservatore Romano*, June 2, 1980.
[68] "A fundamental disquiet", *L'Osservatore Romano*.
[69] *Ibid.*
[70] *Ibid.* Cf. Karol Wojtya, *Milosc i odpowiedzialnosc*, pp. 165-185.

original Covenant with God, the man and woman found themselves, instead of united, more divided or even opposed because of their masculinity and femininity."[71] The fundamental loss of this original unity resulted in "a violation...of the original community-communion of persons"[72] which at the same time caused "the historical man" to undergo the threefold nature of lust: "the lust of the flesh, the lust of the eyes and the pride of life" (J 2:16).[73]

John Paul II's interpretation of the biblical understanding of lust shows that it is "a deception of the human heart in the perennial call of man and woman - a call revealed in the very mystery of creation - to communion by means of mutual giving."[74] The attempt to restore "the original mutual attraction of masculinity and femininity" in man from the "intentional reduction" to simple self-gratification of the body constitutes the historicity of man's process of freeing himself "from pure concupiscence."[75]

In the process of freeing himself from pure concupiscence, man experiences an internal tension between optimism and pessimism: "'Historical' man always evaluates his own 'heart' in his own way, just as he also judges his own 'body,' and so he passes from the pole of pessimism to the pole of optimism."[76] But, since concupiscence is a result of the loss of innocence, man's freedom can be regained by self-control over his desires:

> Concupiscence entails the loss of the interior freedom of the gift. The nuptial meaning of the human body is connected precisely

---

[71] John Paul II, "Dominion over the other in the interpersonal relation", *L'Osservatore Romano*, June 23, 1980; cf. also *idem*, "Lust limits nuptial meaning of the body", *L'Osservatore Romano*, June 30, 1980.
[72] "Dominion over the other", *L'Osservatore Romano*.
[73] Cf. John Paul II, "Sermon on the Mount to the Man of our Day", *L'Osservatore Romano*, August 11, 1980.
[74] "Mutual attraction", *L'Osservatore Romano*.
[75] "Mutual attraction", *L'Osservatore Romano*. Cf. Cardinal S. Wyszynski, "Chrzescijanskie a neopoganskie pojecie kobiety", *Ateneum Kaplanskie*, 3 (1958), pp. 324-336.
[76] "Gospel values", *L'Osservatore Romano*.

with this freedom. Man can become a gift - that is, the man and the woman can exist in the relationship of mutual self-giving - if each of them controls himself.[77]

The final resolution of man's divided desires, then, can come only from his inner self:

> The new dimension of *ethos* is always connected with the revelation of that depth, which is called "heart," and with its liberation from "lust," in order that man, male and female in all the interior truth of the mutual "for," may shine forth more fully in the heart. Freed from the constraint and from the impairment of the spirit that the lust of the flesh brings with it, the human being, male and female, finds himself mutually in the freedom of the gift which is the condition of all life together in truth, and in particular, in the freedom of mutual giving, since both, as husband and wife, must form the sacramental unity willed, as Genesis 2:24 says, by the Creator himself.[78]

IV

The biblical description of man presents human reality not only on a "physical" level as a bodily entity (in Hebrew: *bah-sahr* and in Greek: *sarx*),[79] but also as a psychical (in Hebrew: *neh'-phesh*, and in Greek: *psyche*) and a spiritual (in Hebrew: *rooagh*, and in Greek: *pneuma*) one. In the view of the Bible, this threefold element cannot be separated nor can it be considered as three distinct constituents which are opposed to one another. On the contrary, biblical man is shown to be a unified whole who manifests himself in his three dimensional ontic structure, not as one who constitutes a trichotomic entity.[80]

---

[77] "The 'heart' a battlefield", *L'Osservatore Romano*.

[78] Interpreting the concept of concupiscence", *L'Osservatore Romano*, October 13, 1980.

[79] Cf. John Paul II, "Justification in Christ", *L'Osservatore Romano*, December 29, 1980.

[80] On the three dimensions of man, cf. *ibid.* Cf. also: M. Filipiak, *Biblia*, p. 65f.

Viewing man as a united whole, yet with a threefold dimension to his nature, the Bible stresses that the human being surpasses all other created things: "In fact, it had been marked, so to speak, as a visible factor of the transcendence in virtue of which man as a person, surpasses the visible world of living things (*animalia*)."[81] The transcendentality of biblical man can be seen in various ways, but particularly in the following: man in his spirituality, his divine image and his conscience.

God's solicitous activity in creating man is evidenced by the fact that human nature is ontologically distinct from every other creature in the world. Conceived as a person, man is not only elevated beyond all the other creatures, but is also capable of establishing a communion with other human persons:

> Man's solitude in the Yahwist narrative, is presented to us not only as the first discovery of the characteristic transcendence peculiar to the person, but also as the discovery of an adequate relationship "to" the person, and therefore as an opening and expectation of a "communion of persons."[82]

Therefore, the transcendental structure of man consists of a double solitude: "the communion of persons could be formed only on the basis of a 'double solitude' of man and woman, that is, as their meaning in their 'distinction' from the world of living beings (*animalia*), which gave them both the possibility of being and existing in a special reciprocity."[83] The body, then becomes the "visible" side of human transcendency which carries "the 'image and likeness' of God not only through his own humanity, but also through the communion of persons."[84]

Stressing the divine origin and the transcendental characteristics of the human body, the Bible is "far from

---

[81] "Real significance", *L'Osservatore Romano*.
[82] "By the communion", *L'Osservatore Romano*.
[83] *Ibid.*
[84] *Ibid.*

Manichaeism."[85] In John Paul II's view "the Manichaean interpretation aims at condemnation of the body, as the source of evil, since the 'ontological' principle of evil, according to Manichaeism, is concealed and at the same time manifested in it."[86] The complete "affirmation of the body" prevents the Bible from treating man as an "abnormal mixture of spirit and matter, good and evil."[87] Consequently:

> a Manichaean attitude would lead to an "annihilation" of the body - if not real, at least intentional - to negation of the value of the sex, of the masculinity and femininity of the human person, or at least to their mere "toleration" in the limits of the "needs" delimited by the necessity of procreation for the Manichaean mentality, the body and sexuality constitute, so to speak, an "anti-value."[88]

On the contrary, for Christianity, the "Manichaean way of understanding and evaluating man's body and sexuality is essentially alien to the Gospel, not in conformity with the exact meaning of the words of the Sermon on the Mount spoken by Christ."[89] In conclusion, we refer to Ricoeur who describes Freud, Marx and Nietzsche as the "masters of suspicion,"[90] as John Paul II has remarked:

> In the Nietzschean interpretation, the judgment and accusation of the human heart corresponds, in a way to what is called in biblical language "the pride of life"; in the Marxist interpretation, to what was called "the lust of the eyes"; in the Freudian interpretation, on the other hand, to what is called "the lust of the flesh." The convergence of these conceptions with the interpretation of man found in the Bible lies in the fact that, discovering the three forms of lust in the human heart, we, too, could have limited ourselves to putting that heart in a state of continual suspicion. However, the Bible does not allow us to stop

---

[85] "Depersonalizing", *L'Osservatore Romano*.
[86] "Gospel values", *L'Osservatore Romano*.
[87] *Ibid.*
[88] "Realization", *L'Osservatore Romano*.
[89] *Ibid.*
[90] P. Ricoeur, *Le conflit des interprétations* (Paris: Editions du Seuil, 1969), p. 149.

here. The words of Christ according to Matthew 5:27-28 are such that, while manifesting the whole reality of desire and lust, they do not permit us to make this lust the absolute criterion of anthropology and ethics, that is, the very core of the hermeneutics of man.[91]

The Christian hermeneutics of man accepts a complete "affirmation of the body" and evaluates it positively as a "manifestation of the spirit."[92] John Paul II indicates that the body as the manifestation of spirit, can be found in the fact of incarnated love:

> The human body in its original masculinity and femininity according to the mystery of creation - as we know from the analysis of Genesis 2:23-25 - is not only a source of fertility, that is, of procreation, but right "from the beginning" has a nuptial character: that is to say, it is capable of expressing the love with which the man-person becomes a gift, thus fulfilling the deep meaning of his being and his existence. In this peculiarity, the body is the expression of the spirit and is called, in the very mystery of creation, to exist in the communion of persons "in the image of God."[93]

The incarnated love of man and woman is the transparency of the spirit in their bodies and as it is realized in their mutual look:

> A look expresses what is in the heart. A look expresses, I would say, the man within. If in general it is maintained that man "acts according to his lights" (*operari sequitur esse*), Christ in this case wants to bring out that the man "looks" in conformity with what he is: *intueri sequitur esse*. In a certain sense, man by his look reveals himself to the outside and to others; above all he reveals what he perceives on the "inside."[94]

Presenting man as a person, the Bible reveals him at the same time to be a "partner of the Absolute":

---

[91] "Power of Redeeming completes power of Creation", *L'Osservatore Romano*, November 3, 1980.
[92] "Realization", *L'Osservatore Romano*.
[93] "The 'heart' a battlefield", *L'Osservatore Romano*.
[94] "Concupiscence as a separation from matrimonial significance of the body", *L'Osservatore Romano*, September 15, 1980.

This man, about whom the narrative in the first chapter says that he was created "in the image of God," is manifested in the second narrative <u>as subject of the Covenant,</u> that is, a subject constituted as a person, constituted in the dimension of "<u>partner of the Absolute,</u>" since he must consciously discern and choose between good and evil, between life and death. The words of the first order of God-Yahweh (Gen 2:15-17), which speak directly of the submission and dependence of man the creature on his Creator, indirectly reveal precisely this level of humanity, as subject of the Covenant and "partner of the Absolute."[95]

Although by having a body man participates in the created world, he does not belong entirely to the visible world. In the Bible this fact is described as God's care that man is alone: "Man is 'alone': <u>that means that</u> he, through his own humanity, through what he is, is constituted at the same time in a <u>unique, exclusive and unrepeatable relationship with God Himself.</u>"[96] This special relationship to God comes from the divine image according to which man has been created. By receiving the image of divine nature, man became *participes Creatoris*, and as such "he shares in God's thought and His Law."[97] But as a participant with the Creator Himself, man must do justice to God by respecting His Law: "Justice towards God consists of two elements: respect and safekeeping of the laws of nature, and acknowledgement of the value of a person."[98]

Man receives the axiological meaning of his existence in the form of divine love. In a negative sense, man receives the axiological meaning from "non-identification of his own humanity with the world of living beings (*animalia*) that surround him."[99] The positive axiological meaning of divine love comes, first of all, from God Himself:

---

[95] "Man's awareness", *L'Osservatore Romano*.
[96] *Ibid.*
[97] *Milosc i odpowiedzialnosc*, p. 240.
[98] *Ibid.*
[99] "Fulness", *L'Osservatore Romano*.

Where there is joy, springing from the good, there is love - And only where there is love, is there the joy that comes from the good. The book of Genesis, right from its first chapters, reveals to us God who is Love (although this expression will be used much later by St. John). He is Love, because He rejoices in the good. Creation is, therefore, at the same time a real giving: where there is love, there is giving.[100]

Secondly, the ability to love which man receives from God also makes him free: "It can be said that, created by Love, that is, endowed in their being with masculinity and femininity, they are both 'naked,' because they are real with the very freedom of the gift."[101]

The freedom of love, however, calls for "mastery of oneself" which enables man to "'give himself,' in order that he may become a gift, in order that (...) he will be able to 'fully discover his true self' in 'a sincere giving of himself'."[102] The axiological meaning of freedom of love so conceived is "the 'pure' value of humanity" which enables "human body to reveal(s) not only its masculinity and femininity on the physical plane, but reveals also such a value and such a beauty as to go beyond the purely physical dimension of sexuality."[103] Furthermore, to properly understand the freedom of love, we must see it as "the disinterested gift of oneself - precisely that gift enables them both, man and woman, <u>to find one another,</u> since the Creator willed each of them 'for his (her) own sake'."[104]

Being willed by God, man received a special destiny. Referring to the Conciliar Constitution *Gaudium et Spes*, John Paul II writes: "Man, indeed, as a person is 'the only creature on earth that God has willed for its own sake' and, at the same

---

[100] "Creation", *L'Osservatore Romano*.
[101] John Paul II, "The man-person becomes a gift in the freedom of love", *L'Osservatore Romano*, January 21, 1980.
[102] *Ibid*.
[103] "Creation as fundamental and original gift", *L'Osservatore Romano*, January 7, 1980.
[104] "The man-person", *L'Osservatore Romano*.

time he is the one who 'can fully discover his true self only by a sincere giving of himself'."[105] The special dignity of man consists of his conscience through which he can master himself:

> that he should be able to obey correct conscience; to be the true master of his own deep impulses, like a guardian who watches over a hidden spring, and finally to draw from all those impulses what is fitting for "purity of heart," building with conscience and consistency that personal sense of the nuptial meaning of the body which opens the interior space of the freedom of the gift.[106]

By following his conscience, man can reach:

> that deeper and more mature spontaneity with which his heart, mastering his instincts, rediscovers the spiritual beauty of the sign constituted by the human body in its masculinity and femininity.[107]

The conscience is the very core of "human inner life,"[108] the "deepest forces of the heart"[109] and the foundation for the "transformation of Christian ethos."[110] The fact of human conscience is evident in the divine commandment to obey God (Gen. 3:2-3), in the law of marriage and family (Gen. 2:23-24), in respecting the private property (Gen. 1:28-30), etc.[111] Although the Bible derives the human conscience mainly from the original sin "as a fruit of the tree of the knowledge of good and evil,"[112] nevertheless, it becomes "the most secret core and sanctuary of man, where he finds himself alone with God, whose voice can be heard in his inmost being...."[113]

---

[105] "The 'heart'", *L'Osservatore Romano*.
[106] "Spontaneity", *L'Osservatore Romano*. Cf. Karol Wojtyla, *Fruitful and Responsible Love* (New York: The Seabury Press, 1979), pp. 27-32.
[107] "Spontaneity", *L'Osservatore Romano*.
[108] John Paul II, "Meaning of adultery transferred from the body to the heart", *L'Osservatore Romano*, September 8, 1980.
[109] "Concupiscence as a separation", *L'Osservatore Romano*.
[110] "Realization", *L'Osservatore Romano*.
[111] Cf. W. Poplatek, *Istota sumienia wedlug Pisma Swietego*, (Lublin: Towarzystwo Naukowe KUL), 1961.
[112] John Paul II, "Meaning of original human experiences", *L'Osservatore Romano*.
[113] Karol Wojtyla, *Sign of Contradiction*, p. 140.

II. ON THE MEANING OF MARRIAGE

The biblical vision of man is—according to John Paul II—a dynamic one, and it expresses a profound truth of the mystery of human existence which can be resolved in love:

> Man cannot live without love. He remains a being that is incomprehensible for himself, his life is senseless, if love is not revealed to him, if he does not encounter love, if he does not experience it and make it his own, if he does not participate intimately in it. This, as has already been said, is why Christ the Redeemer "fully reveals man to himself" (II,10).[1]

Before exploring the Christian view of marriage, let us establish the role of love in human existence.

I

John Paul II, referring to St. Thomas' doctrine on values, says that the human existence of each and every individual man reveals the dignity in love:

> Above all, Love is greater than sin, than weakness, than the vanity of creation; it is stronger than death; it is Love always ready to raise up and forgive; always ready to go to meet the prodigal son; always looking for "the revealing of the sons of God" who are called to the glory, that is to be revealed. This revelation of love is also described as charity; and in man's history this revelation of love and charity has taken a form and a name: that of Jesus Christ (II,9).[2]

In view of this text, John Paul II considers the very essence of human life as a specific and unique synthesis of his existence and love. However, in order to properly understand this specific synthesis of man's existence and love, we must view man not only as a part of pure nature, but also and specifically, as a unique person endowed with some special dignity of his own. By maintaining that man receives his dignity as a person by a dynamic process which unifies his existence with love, Karol Wojtyla writes:

> At times, human life seems to be too short for love. At other times, the situation is reversed: human love seems to be too short-lived in relation to human life - or, perhaps, too superficial. In any case, man has at his disposal some kind of existence and some kind of love: how can a sensible unity be made out of these? This wholeness cannot be one that is closed in itself. It has to be open in such a manner, that it is transmitted to other men, mirroring at the same time, the absolute Existence and Love - always mirroring It in some way or other.[3]

Identifying existence and love in man, John Paul II refers first to the Greek experience, especially to the Platonic

---

[2] *Ibid.*
[3] "Przed sklepem jubilera", *Znak* 12 (1960), p. 1605f.

doctrine of *Eros*. For Plato, however, man's nature is split between the spiritual and material world. Being lodged in the body but at the same time also being affected by bodily drives, man's spiritual soul finds itself in a constant tension "between the world of the senses and the world of Ideas, (and) has the destiny of passing from the first to the second."[4] But, since the human soul is imprisoned in the body, it cannot detach itself from the world of senses by Ideas alone. A new question now arises: what is the motive power through which man can overcome this bondage? Plato sees the source and the motive power for passing from the material to the spiritual mode of human existence in *Eros* which is "congenital in man."[5] But Platonic *Eros* is a twofold force: an immanent one through which the soul can communicate and move toward the *eide* and, secondly, a transcendent one through which man can sublimate and return to the world of ideas. In the words of John Paul II:

> When man begins to have a presentiment of Ideas, thanks to contemplation of the objects existing in the world of the senses, he receives the impulse from *Eros*, that is, from the desire for pure Ideas. *Eros*, in fact, is the guiding of the "sensual" or "sensitive" man towards what is transcendent: the force that directs the soul towards the world of Ideas. Plato describes the stages of this influence of *Eros*: the latter raises man's soul from the beauty of a single body to that of all bodies, and so to the beauty of knowledge and finally to the very idea of Beauty.[6]

Platonic *Eros*, conceived as both an immanent and a transcendent force for man's passage from the sensible to the ideal world, is not causalistic but telic in orientation, that is, directed towards the Good. In other words, the ultimate goal of Platonic *Eros* is directed toward reaching the final perfection of the human soul. John Paul II comments:

---

4   "Eros and Ethos meet and bear fruit in the human heart", *L'Osservatore Romano,* November 10, 1980.
5   *Ibid.*
6   *Ibid.*

> *Eros* is neither purely human nor divine: it is something intermediate (*daimonion*) and intermediary. Its principal characteristic is permanent aspiration and desire. Even when it seems to give freely, *Eros* persists as the "desire of possessing," and yet it is different from purely sensual love, being the love that strives towards the sublime. According to Plato, the gods do not love because they do not feel desires, since their desires are all satisfied. Therefore they can only be the object, but not the subject of love (*Symposium 200-201*). So they do not have a direct relationship with man; only the mediation of *Eros* makes it possible for a relationship to be established (*Symposium 203*). *Eros* is, therefore, the way that leads man to divinity, but not *vice versa*. The aspiration to transcendence is, therefore, a constituent element of the Platonic concept of *Eros*, a concept that overcomes the radical dualism of the world of ideas and the world of the senses. *Eros* makes it possible to pass from one to the other. It is therefore a form of escape beyond the material world, which the soul must renounce, because the beauty of the sensible subject has a value only insofar as it leads higher.[7]

Immanent *Eros*, as described by Eryximachus in *Symposium*, consists of a natural attraction of/to everything which is beautiful and good in the whole of reality. This natural attraction is rooted in everything by the desire to obtain and to possess the good sought forever. John Paul II comments:

> According to Plato, "*Eros*" represents the interior force that drags man towards everything good, true and beautiful. This "attraction" indicates, in this case, the intensity of a subjective act of the human spirit. In the common meaning, on the contrary - as also in literature - this "attraction" seems to be first and foremost of a sensual nature. It arouses the mutual tendency of both the man and the woman to draw closer to each other, to the union of bodies, to that union of which Genesis 2:24 speaks...[8]

However, the Platonic *Eros* is a natural desire for 'self-perfection' and the Christian understanding of love is conceived as a supernatural power for justification. In the Christian doctrine, love is called *Agape*, because it is a redemptive power

---

[7] *Ibid.*
[8] *Ibid.*

for salvation. In a word, *Agape* makes man "the *particeps Creatoris* in his thoughts and actions."⁹

II

As a *particeps Creatoris* man is an incarnated being by having body as an object of material nature, and by being body as a subject of spiritual life. In the former, since he is identified with body-object, man is endowed with instinctive power of the material world; hence he is capable of realizing his own existence by relating to and communicating with other being. But, in the latter, since he is a being who is identified with body-subject, man's existence consists in a specific dialectic of a "creative tension between the 'I' and those depths of our being, in and by which we are."¹⁰ These two characteristics of the human body designate to man a twofold destiny of his existence, i.e., as an 'outer-and-inner-oriented-being'.

This twofold destiny of human existence reveals man as both an external and internal being, and one who should, in relation to other persons, avoid them for one's own sake. Rejecting any mode of using other persons for one's own sake, Wojtyla analyzes two principal meanings of the verb 'to use'.

The first meaning describes use as the exercise of an act as a means to an end. This involves subordination, a hierarchy and a set priority of things. In this case, the means is subordinated to the intended end. The initiator of the action and the end he intends subordinate action and it subject in terms of service to them. Man has creation at this disposal to satisfy his ends. This involves minerals, plants and animals. It also entails human persons. The commander may use soldiers to attain

---

[9] Milosc i odpowiedzialnosc (Kraków: *Znak*, 1962), p. 24.
[10] G. Marcel, *Creative Fidelity* (New York: Farrar, Strauss & Giroux, 1964), p. 65.

victory in battle. A man may use a plumber to correct defects in household plumbing. Such actions are valid, since they conform to the principle prohibiting the treatment of persons as mere means to an end. Alluding to the categorical imperative of Kant, Wojtyla goes on to examine the relationship between a man and a woman. The conclusion draw is that, in the realm of sexual ethics, a person cannot be treated as a mere means to an end.

> This is precluded by the very nature of person, by what any person is. For a person is a thinking subject, and capable of making decisions: these, most notably, are the attributes we find in the inner self of a person. Since this is so every person is by nature capable of determining his or her aims. Anyone who treats a person as a means to end does violence to the very essence of the other, to what constitutes its natural right.[11]

Thus, the first meaning of the verb "to use" cannot be applied to the relations between a man and a woman because it destroys each other's personhood, which is grounded in rational deliberation and volitional self-determination.

The second meaning of the verb "to use" is seen as a modification of the first meaning. It concerns itself primarily with the enjoyment of sexual pleasure. This view is very common and involves the sexual relationship between persons. Pleasure, delight and enjoyment are the basic aims of this relationship between two human beings on the physical level. Therefore, "use" equals "enjoy" as a verb. This meaning of use is also invalid for a personal relationship. In this concept, enjoyment is higher than love, which denies authentic personhood of the other. Rather, the acknowledgement of the other as a person results in the exact opposite: "The belief that a human being is a person leads to the acceptance of the postulate that enjoyment must be subordinated to love."[12] Therefore, the sexual relationship must be based on a caring

---

[11] *Milosci i Odpowiedzialnosc*, p. 17.
[12] *Ibid.*, p. 24.

love, or else it will lead to a depersonalizing relationship of self- gratification.

There is now a shift in the thought of the author to a more thorough examination of the nature of sexuality in terms of the sexual urge. Wojtyla differentiates between instinct and urge. Instinct is viewed as "the reflex mode of action, which is not dependent on conscious thought."[13] Man, in relation to his instincts, is "by nature capable of rising above instinct in his actions."[14]

Urge is very close to instinct in meaning but somewhat different. Wojtyla describes it as "a certain orientation, a certain direction in man's life implicit in his nature."[15] The author then goes on to conclude that there is a sexual urge rather than sexual instinct. This sexual urge is seen as "a natural drive born in all human beings, a vector of aspiration along which their whole existence develops and perfects itself from within."[16] After expressing the fact that the sexual urge is not the source of actions but rather a human property that is expressed in actions, Wojtyla critically evaluates various interpretations of human sexuality, especially, the religious, rigorist and 'libidinistic' explanations.

The religious interpretation of human sexuality is connected with Judeo-Christian doctrine of creation, conceived in terms of conservation which, according to Wojtyla, consists in a continuous process of procreation. In other words, creation is a continuous process of sustaining of that which is already created, and that which can be brought into existence. In the view of the Cardinal of Kraków, man and woman participate in this continuing "cosmic stream by which existence is

---

[13] *Ibid.*, p. 35.
[14] *Ibid.*, p. 36.
[15] *Ibid.*
[16] *Ibid.*

transmitted"[17] by the activity of procreation. In procreation, a human being is brought into the world and thus follows God's plan of creation. It is the sexual union between man and woman which creates the human body which is ensouled and becomes a human person. Parents, therefore, contribute to the creation of the person by God. The parents continue to participate in the creation of the person through education and love. Wojtyla then formulates the goal of the sexual urge in terms of the religious interpretation: "Procreation is the proper end of the sexual urge which - as was said before - simultaneously furnishes material for love between persons, male and female."[18] The connection between God and this sexual urge is explained by the author in the following way: "The sexual urge is connected in a special way with the natural order of existence, which is the divine order inasmuch as it is realized under the continuous influence of God the Creator."[19]

III

From the religious evaluation of sexual activity of man, it follows its ethico-moral character. Archbishop Kevin McNamara observes:

> According to Catholic teaching - and Catholic teaching in general - an action is morally good if it fits within the framework of God's plan for humanity, if it is consistent with accepting God's offer of eternal life with the Blessed Trinity in and through Christ Our Lord. It is morally evil if, in any way, it falls outside these limits.[20]

The interrelation between the religious and moral dimension of human sexuality requires some specific criterion

---

[17] *Ibid.*, p. 44.
[18] *Ibid.*, p. 45.
[19] *Ibid.*, p. 46.
[20] "Law and Morality", *L'Osservatore Romano*, December 22-29, 1986.

which would allow the formation of a proper judgment as to which sexual behavior is correct and good, and which one is reproachful and evil.

In the historical development of the Catholic Church, one can differentiate two main attitudes in moral theology. One stresses the purpose of man's activity; the other emphasizes the normative (i.e. value-oriented) character of human behavior. For example, the distinction between purpose-oriented and norm (or value)-oriented moral theology poses far-reaching consequences for Catholic teaching on human sexuality.

On the one hand, if human sexuality is mainly viewed from the point of its purpose, then the emphasis is given to the act of procreation. Because the very nature of the sexual act aims ultimately at reproduction of the species as such, the purpose-orientation underestimates the need for personal fulfillment of the spouses.

On the other hand, if the emphasis is given to the normative, as opposed to the instinctive character of man's sexual activity, then its morality recognizes the persons involved as fundamentally valuable. This view emphasizes that only human individuals constitute the highest of inherent goodness and, consequently, the natural forces should be subordinated to personal ones.

In traditional Catholic moral theology on human sexuality, the emphasis was made on the purpose of man's sexuality, which gives emphasis to the instinctive forces. This interpretation was greatly influenced by Aristotelian and Thomistic teleological ethics. Such an attitude, by overemphasizing the natural forces of man's sexuality, prompted Catholic moral theologians to make a radical distinction between the primary (procreation) and secondary (mutual "love") purposes of marriage. Thus the traditional attitude toward marriage became deterministic in nature and utilitarian in character. In other words, this belief of purpose of marriage leads inevitably to the subjection of human sexuality to the blind forces of nature, and to the viewing of living persons related to each other by love, as useful objects of mere sexual self-gratification.

The humanistic philosophy of Karol Wojtyla led him to a distinctly different view of the morality of human sexuality. The Cardinal from Kraków attempts to make a synthesis between a normative and purpose-oriented moral theology, basing it on personalistic principle. In view of the fact that man and woman are persons, in sexual expression of their love they should consciously realize both self-completion of their nature and they should actively engage themselves in participation in *opus creationis* of a new life. In the words of Wojtyla: "Sexual morality consists in a constant and mature synthesis of the purpose of nature and personalistic norm."[21]

On the one hand, if the satisfaction of the human sexual instinct becomes an exclusive foundation of marriage, it will inevitably end in a total depersonalization of the spouses and lead to the destruction of spiritual life of their marriage. The abuses in the sphere of sexuality are almost irreversible. But, on the other hand, if the sexual instinct is used exclusively for procreation, the spouses become only a means for the blind forces of nature, thus depriving them from mutual fulfillment of their personal nature.

Wojtyla criticizes all forms of "using persons" which is so prevalent in contemporary ethical practices. He reiterates the personalistic norm which holds that persons can never be the object of use or exploitation. If love is properly understood, it always carries with it a concomitant note of deep responsibility: "Responsibility for love of a person is here augmented by the responsibility for his/her life and health

---

[21] *Milosc i Odpowiedzialnosc*, p. 56f.

which constitute a 'weave' of basic goods deciding on the ethical value of each factor of marital relationship."[22]

Responsible love then becomes the foundation for "responsibility for life in which definite values find their realization."[23] Basing love on the act of responsibility, the existence of the other person for me becomes a mutual gift "that embraces the human being as a whole, soul and body."[24]

Responsible love is fulfilled in a fruitful parenthood. The reason for this is that "in the sexual relationship between man and woman, two orders meet: the order of nature, which has as its object reproduction, and the personal order, which finds its expression in the love of persons and aims at the fullest realization of that love."[25] Therefore, by the very fact of sexual activity the spouses enter into a participation in the function of the order of nature: "A man and a woman who, as husband and wife, unite in a full sexual relationship thereby enter into the realm of what can properly be called the order of nature."[26] Sexual intercourse between husband and wife, which deliberately excludes the possibility of their becoming parents, has a "non full objective justification."[27] Moreover, the rejection of the possibility of becoming parents while the spouses are engaged in sexual intercourse "conflicts not only with the order of nature but with love itself."[28] Finally, an attempt to separate sexuality from parenthood is a violation of God's intention and His Will: "Man is just towards God when he recognizes the order of nature and conforms his actions to it."[29]

---

[22] *Ibid.*, p. 219.
[23] *Fruitful and Responsible Love* (New York: The Seabury 1979), p. 20.
[24] *Ibid.*
[25] *Milosc i Odpowiedzialnosc*, p. 220.
[26] *Ibid.*, p. 219.
[27] *Ibid.*, p. 222.
[28] *Ibid.*, p. 230.
[29] *Ibid.*, p. 240.

Summarizing his teaching on conjugal love and fruitful parenthood, Wojtyla compares the relative importance of freedom and love:

> Only truth about oneself can bring about a real engagement of one's freedom in relations with another person. It is a giving of oneself; it means a limitation of one's freedom for the sake of another person. Freedom is for love. Unused by love, it becomes something negative, leaving man with an emptiness and a lack of fulfillment. Love engages freedom, filling it with that which nature itself desires: it fills it with goodness . . . man needs love more than he needs freedom, since freedom is only a means, whereas love is a purpose.[30]

IV

The very core of sexual morality is a love which is based on the personalistic principle. In order to become fully human, then, is to become more a person by fostering love. Without love, man can neither be himself nor discover the truth of his personal destiny. Wojtyla's existential personalism offers trustworthy insights into the basic structure of human nature with all the possibility of man conceived as a person.

The question arises: what is the meaning for man to be a person? The person "differs from a thing in structure and in degree of perfection."[31] Structure refers to the inner subjective self that constitutes the spiritual element of man as found in the soul. The degree of perfection concerns itself with the spiritual perfectibility that man strives for by nature. It is this spiritual element of man in his soul that comprises the value of his personhood. The degree of perfectibility shows him to be more than just an animated body and hence it distinguishes him from the animal kingdom.

---

[30] *Ibid.*, p. 124.
[31] *Ibid.*, p. 110.

When we define man as a person in terms of his perfectibility, the human being is conceived here as a dynamic subject, which is constituted of acts through which an individual manifests his own inner self. He thus becomes "the root-factor of his human action (which) involves the specific interplay of the personal system" of any individual man.[32] But in the case of "man-person", conceived as a subject who manifests himself through his acts, his nature is identified with what he is experiencing: "Thus in every human experience there is also a certain measure of understanding of what is experienced."[33]

Man expresses his human experience as a 'person-act' through sensation and emotions. The distinction between sensations and emotions Wojtyla describes as follows:

> Sensations are to be differentiated from emotions. Sensations can also be a sensual reaction to a subject: the content of a sensation differs widely from that of emotion. In the content of sensation the image of the object is reflected; in emotion, we experience its value. We must consider here the fact that different objects, with which we are coming into sensual contact, draw our attention not only to their content, but also to their value as well. Sensations denote a reaction to content; emotions, a reaction to value.[34]

Human existence then can be identified with experiencing one's own value as a person. However, in experiencing one's own value as a person, man becomes conscious of some feelings, or, in other words, in experiencing one's own self, man realizes that his emotional feelings reveal to him something which is discovered as values. Commenting on Max Scheler's notion of *Wert-Fühlen* Cardinal Wojtyla writes:

> The experience proper to moral values is similar to the experience proper to all other values through value-feeling (*Wert-*

---

[32] "The Intentional Act and the Human Act that is, Act and Experience," *Analecta Husserliana*, 5 (1976), p. 170.
[33] *Osoba i czyn* (Kraków: Polskie Towarzystwo Teologiczne, 1985), p. 14.
[34] *Milosc i odpowiedzialnosc*, p. 91.

Fühlen). <u>Only in the feeling of values,</u> all kinds of values, including the moral, appear in their own proper essence. That appearance of values in feeling is not a form of producing them by the subject, by man. It is only a discovery of values in an objective reality. Values are 'material' or 'objectively intrinsic'.[35]

In the very structure of experiencing emotions, these values are not produced but discovered by man in his 'feeling-experience'. Now in experiencing one's own emotions, man finds a specific "hierarchy of values."[36] This hierarchy of values is real in nature and objective in character, because they are revealing the authenticity of "the content of human experience."[37] The reason for this authenticity of "the content of human experience" is the fact that it is not just an intentional act it expresses but the real character of human feelings.[38] The human experience of 'value-feeling', therefore, "reveals at the same time the dynamic reality of the subject, man who acts, who performs the act. <u>Already through the very act is being manifested</u> adequately the <u>subject's ability to act</u>."[39]

The manifestation of the authentic experience of "value-feeling" can only take place through love, because love is the highest value of man, by which a human being can become fully a person. But, since man's nature is composed of body and soul, then human love must be an integrated love. Integrated love, which entails the sexual value of the person with the value of the person as such, it subordinates the former to the latter and affirms the person as person.

This affirmation of an integrated love constitutes love as a virtue. In this case it is not merely an emotion because it involves the giving of one person to another: "This virtue is produced in the will and has at its disposal the resources of the

---

[35] "The Intentional Act", p. 271.
[36] *Ibid.*, p. 272.
[37] *Ibid.*, p. 273.
[38] *Ibid.*, p. 275.
[39] *Ibid.*, p. 277.

will's spiritual potential: in other words, it is an authentic commitment of the free will of one person (the subject), resulting from the truth about another person (the object)."[40]

After this analysis of the relation of love and its affirmation of the person, Wojtyla concludes with the following conception of love as a virtue: "Love as a virtue is oriented by the will towards the value of the person."[41] This is the formulation of the central idea of the ethical analysis. Succinctly stated, Wojtyla's definition is of a twofold nature. One pertains to the will as that faculty of man's soul exercised in the act of human love. The other focuses on the value of the person and one's perception of it which is the starting point of integrated love. In the words of Wojtyla: "The will, then, is the source of that affirmation of the person which permeates all the reactions, all the feelings, the whole behavior of the subject."[42]

Integrated love which is based on will power and the value of person, enables Wojtyla to establish a proper relationship between two persons who are mutually in love. One, with his will, gives himself to the other and in this process removes the inviolable aspect of the human person. The person, therefore, "surrenders himself to another, to the one he loves."[43] This surrender forgoes one's autonomy for the higher good of the beloved and it also makes a gift of one's self to the other who is loved.

> Love proceeds by way of this renunciation, guided by the profound conviction that it does not diminish and impoverish, but quite the contrary, enlarges and enriches the existence of the person...the lover 'goes outside' the self to find a fuller existence in another.[44]

---

[40] *Milosc i odpowiedzialnosc*, p. 112.
[41] *Ibid.*
[42] *Ibid.*
[43] *Ibid.*, p. 114.

V

After laying the metaphysical foundation of the ethico-moral aspect of love, it is necessary to focus on the ultimate purpose of love. According to Wojtyla the final goal of love is 'self-realization':

> It should be stressed here that love is the fullest realization of these potentialities with which man is endowed. This potentiality (from the Latin: *potentia*: possibility, ability, power) proper to a person is, to the fullest, actualized through love (actualize from Latin: *actus*: act, perfection). A person finds in love the fullness of his being, of his objective existing. Love means that particular action, that particular act, which expands to the fullest the existence of a person. It must be, of course, a true love. What is true love? True love is a love in which the real essence of love is being realized--love which turns towards the real (not just a seeming) good in a real manner, i.e., in a manner which conforms to its nature. This can also be applied to love between man and woman. In this area also, true love perfects and develops personal existence. A false love, on the other hand, has contrary results. False love turns toward false good, and --what happens more often--to some actual real good, but in a manner which does not conform to its nature, or even opposes it... A false love is an evil love.[45]

Love, then, is the ultimate and fundamental principle of "self-realization" of man as a "person-act" and, as such, "has above all, a metaphysical character."[46] But the metaphysical character of love points "to the objective integrity of a person and to the demands of personalistic norms contained in it."[47] Love, however, analyzed from the metaphysical point of view is not, by itself, a simple moral norm; it is a real virtue, i.e., a moral disposition to goodness.

---

[45] *Ibid.*, p. 71.
[46] *Ibid.*, p. 84.
[47] *Ibid.*, p. 57.

Love as a virtue becomes the ontological foundation through which an individual person can realize his/her own human existence. But love considered as a virtue also becomes the ultimate value through which an individual person realizes his own happiness: "Love demands an affirmation of the value of a person. Basing itself on this affirmation, the will of the subject who loves, strives for the good of the person loved--for a full and total good. Such a good is identified with happiness."[48]

Moreover, in this maturing process towards the fullness of someone's existence, love considered as a virtue directs the individual person towards an "other-fellow-person," realizing, thereby, the insufficiency of oneself and the need for the other as other. Furthermore, a true love, as an other-oriented motive power for 'self-fulfillment,' cannot use or exploit the other person: "This attitude of the will of the person who loves, is in strict opposition to any attitude of the will directed towards using the other person. Love and relating to a person as an object to be used mutually exclude themselves."[49]

Every genuine love is completely disinterested: "Love excludes self-interest; love is disinterested in its very essence; it is even more unconditionally disinterested than justice."[50]

In conclusion, love is the ultimate and fundamental principle of self-actualization of man as a "person-act." This occurs when man realizes "the real good in a real manner, i.e., in a manner which conforms to his nature."[51] Moreover, love as the motive power of the realization of goodness in man is also "perfecting and developing (his) personal existence."[52] But love, being "good-oriented" is, by the same token, not only the

---

[48] *Ibid.*, p. 174.
[49] *Ibid.*
[50] "Problem bezinteresownosci," *Tygodnik Powszechny* 34 (1957).
[51] *Milosc i odpowiedzialnosc*, p. 71.
[52] *Ibid.*

fundamental principle of integrity of "man-person" in the order of all his actions, but it is also the ultimate end of human activity, constituting thus a proper axiological hierarchy of human *praxis*.

III. ON THE CONCEPT OF CATHOLIC EDUCATION

In the spirit of responsibility for spreading the Good News among the nations in all times, the bringing up of new generations of faithful, is one of the main concerns of the apostolic work of the church. However, in view of the fact of the differences between generations, on the one hand, and the constant changes of socio-cultural life, on the other hand, the process of upbringing new generation creates many problems and requires a need for constant search of finding a proper balance between two different environments. One, created by his family with its specific experience and traditions, the other created by the surrounding society. These constant transitions from one environment to the other is naturally a source of growing conflicts and misunderstanding, especially for the young. In order to find the balance between these two standards of values, one must search for new evaluation of the existing situation.

The purpose of this essay is to re-think Catholic teaching on the goal and foundation of education both from the philosophical and theological tradition of the Western Christianity. Studying Christian doctrine on education one can also appreciate the apostolic zeal of the Church in spreading both the secular and sacral knowledge in the spirit of Revelation.

I

The problem of the so-called generation gap is not a new issue and in reality can be considered as a constitutive factor of each generation. If the process of bringing up children means to prepare them for their future independence and develop their abilities to formulate their own ideas, then sooner or later the moment of a break-away from their parents, will necessarily have to take place. A generation gap thus understood has to be regarded as a normal process; a process necessary for the young in their growth to maturity, responsibility and self-reliance. History of sociology proves that in certain periods of history this gap acquires a drastic intensity. The break-away from parents often takes on a form of rejection and destruction of all the existing ties and links between generations.

The most characteristic aspect of today's generation gap is its universality both in its contents and scope. In its contents it denotes a total lack of any need for the cultural life of the past. The new generation of today is facing the possibility of a total rejection of all cultural values inherited from their forefathers, regardless of the fact that they constitute one of the basic elements of growth of any generation. As the most vivid example of this attitude we witness the hippies movement with their motto to "do their own thing". The other puzzling and unsettling aspect of today's generation gap is its scope. It must be evident to every serious-minded person that this gap has already reached a destructive and radical form.

A breach between generations as such does not stem from the human nature itself, but is basically connected with the cultural life of a society, and as such belongs to the phenomenon related to education. The proper laws of nature demand a certain sense of solidarity and mutual respect between parents and their children. Directed by the law of love, the parents desire to transmit to their children all they consider to be of great value. Yet this implantation of values can only take place in and through a process of bringing up and raising children. And that requires both dedication and sacrifice on both sides. The lack of those elements lead to the present permissiveness. Unfortunately too often the modern methods of raising children leave much to be desired, both in the area of bringing up and in educating.

The generation gap in regards to cultural life consists mainly on the discontinuation of values. In the times of sudden and basic cultural changes this discontinuation takes on the characteristics of serious conflict. It is sufficient to refer to history and the changes which took place at the end of medieval times. The well-known Dutch philosopher and historian, Huizinga in his book *The Waning of the Middle Ages* notes the same occurrences which happened at that time, and which resemble some of the contemporary hippie movements such as The Brothers of the Common Table which remind us of today's communes. The constant migration which lead to the uprooting of many people from the social life, caused numerous wars and tensions between different nations. The feeling of uneasiness and dissatisfaction which then arose as a result brought on the rejection of the entire cultural system. J.J. Rousseau, the father of naturalism, directly blamed culture for the existing crisis and called for the return to nature. All of these movements finally lead to the French Revolution and the overthrow of the European feudal system. Out of the cinders of the Revolution a new image of the world has been born: the world of technology and production. Nations, as well as private individuals became rich and powerful. The cult of money grew to absurdity. The field of business and industry with their tempting possibilities drew entire cadres of scientists, depriving the universities of the ever needed professors.

In order to find a proper balance between the old and the new generations one has to stress the role of education. Complying with the updated need for education one has to postulate the principle of integration, both on the individual, social, national and cultural level. This postulate corresponds with the multi-faced integrity of human interaction. First of all an individual being is that which St. Thomas Aquinas called the most perfect in the whole nature. As the most perfect being in all nature, the individual person is unique and as such demands absolute and total respect. Even for the 'highest goodness' he must remain intact both in his individuality and personality.

As a unique and unrepeatable person, the individual man is interconnected with other fellow-beings. In this respect he is organically interwoven with a given society in which he is living and constantly interacting with fellow men. This social dimension of man is not established by nature but depends on the current basic demands and requirements of the surrounding social conditions. These dimensions of sociability of man require a systematic process of education.

However, both the individual and social need for spiritual exercise and spiritual values would be ineffective should they fail to represent and integrate the cultural values. Thus we arrive at the most essential element of education. This element constitutes the most universal human endeavors in spiritual life of any individual. However, this individual spiritual need is only a reflection of the universal values as such.

The individual and the national values can receive their validity only if they are interconnected and blend with the general human cultural values. Finally then, we can postulate the cultural integration. This postulate presumes the shift, at least in some respect, from the need of a prestige-type sphere of material values to cultural ones.

II

Education is, according to Vatican II, one of the basic natural rights and the most universal privilege of every human person.[1] Now, in view of the duality of human reality as *homo natura* and *homo persona*, Catholic teaching proclaims that education should aim at fostering the supernatural life and divine grace received in the Sacrament of Baptism. The Fathers of the Council write in the "Declaration on Christian Education":

> Since every Christian has become a new creature by rebirth from water and the Holy Spirit, so that he may be called what he truly is, a child of God, he is entitled to a Christian education. Such an education does not merely strive to foster in the human person the maturity already described. Rather, its principal aims are these: that as the baptized person is gradually introduced into a knowledge of the mystery of salvation, he may daily grow more conscious of the gift of faith which he has received...[2]

Christian education, however, cannot limit itself to the supernatural life of divine grace only, but it should also aim towards "promoting the Christian transformation of the world by which natural values, viewed in the full perspective of humanity as redeemed by Christ, may contribute to the good of society as a whole."[3] The biblical keyword for "the Christian transformation of the World", is *metanoia*, meaning inner transformation of the individual soul and conversion of man to

---

[1] Cf. "Declaration on Christian Education", in *The Documents of Vatican II*, ed. by Walter M. Abbott (New York: Guild Press, 1966), p. 638.
[2] *Ibid.*, p. 640.
[3] *Ibid.*

new life in Christ by conducting himself according to the spirit that gives him divine grace.[4] Consequently the Christian notion of education is not limited only to the immanent order of natural self-perfection of the individual man, but it aims at the transcendent order of divine redemption of the whole mankind, both horizontally and vertically.

The etymology of the term 'education' indicates in its Latin derivatives two meanings: 'meaning-content' (*educo, -are*) - 'to train', 'to produce', and 'meaning-value' (*educo, -ere*) - 'to raise up', 'to bear'. In 'bringing-up' then the young generation, education must aim at unfolding of all potentialities of each individual person. In other words, in the process of unfolding of all human potentialities, there is in education a dialectical tension between objective and subjective interests and capacities of each individual man. Now, in education so considered, we may distinguish the two-fold unfolding of one's innate potentialities which can be formulated as essential (or 'objective') and existential (or 'subjective'). The essential attitude attempts to subordinate the subjective over and against the objective *ap*-prehension in the following way: from objective perceptions through subjective recollections, back to objective cognition. The existential attitude on the other hand attempts to reverse this process and in subordinating the objective to the subjective elements it proclaims the superiority of personal self-*com*-prehension in the following way: from subjective apperception through objective cognition, back to subjective self-understanding.

Education, understood as a process of unfolding of one's all personal interests and individual capacities requires searching for a balance between essential needs and existential demands in knowing (*ap*-prehension of reality from without) and understanding (*com*-prehension of reality from within), according to

---

[4] Cf. Rudolf Schnackenburg, *Christian Existence in the New Testament* (Notre Dame: University of Notre Dame Press, 1968), p. 55.

the principle: the broader the range of our knowledge, the deeper our self-understanding. Should any balance be disturbed between inner and outer knowledge and understanding, overspecialization by exclusive concentration on one particular aspect of knowledge or simple diletantism will ensue. In order to avoid the danger of both, overspecialization and simplistic diletantism, education should provide and encourage searching for truth in its integrity and totality. The father of our Western cultural life, Nicolas Copernicus, who was both a great scientist and humanist, expressed the spirit of education as "the search for truth in all and everything."[5]

Integrity and totality as the ultimate goal of education is nothing but the essential condition for full involvement, not only of our intellect, but also and especially, of our will and emotions. Education based on integrity and totality in "searching for truth in all and everything" would consist in a spiritual transformation which by the early Christianity was understood as the adopted from the Greek expression *metanoia*. The Christian understanding of *metanoia* aims at a spiritual transformation both as regards toward contemplation of truth and as regards the concrete actions of everyday life according to the axiom: "*contemplata aliis tradere.*" Now, education based on *metanoia* of our outer activity is cause-oriented, and as such aims towards revelation of truth hidden in reality through which man can realize God's commandment: "Be fruitful, and multiply; fill the earth and subdue it" (Gen. 1:28). Education, however, based on *metanoia* of our inner contemplation of truth is end-oriented and as such aims at inspiration towards truth through which one can obtain, or at least begin to participate even in this life, in the beatific vision, as expressed by St. Thomas Aquinas: "Thus the whole perfection to which soul can attain according to philosophers consists in that the whole order of the universe will be described in it and all their causes.

---

[5] *De Revolutionibus* (Thoruni, 1873), p. 3.

In this also they put the ultimate end of man, which according to us will be in vision of God."[6]

Education conceived as both revelation of truth and inspiration towards truth is the very destiny and purpose of human activity, through which man extends himself as "*quasi in horizonte existens aeternitatis et temporis.*"[7] Education, then, as a spiritual *metanoia* transforms individual persons from within and engages him in a transfiguration of the divinely created world. In this sense St. Thomas Aquinas, following Aristotle, said: "*Humanum genus arte et ratione vivit.*"[8] *Ars* meaning art and technology as creating the temporal mode of becoming human, and *ratio* meaning science and morality, as creating eternal mode of being man. Now, this two-fold character of education as spiritual *metanoia* indicates that revelation of truth and inspiration towards truth consists in unrestricted cultivation of all and every human value. Practically speaking every individual should be exposed to a set of higher values, be they scientific or spiritual, such as justice, honesty, compassion, responsibility, equality, etc., in both professional and personal life.

In cultivating higher values, education must provide unrestricted and unlimited freedom, but in the spirit of personal responsibility. As a matter of fact, authentic freedom provides self-control and personal restraint in appropriating genuine values. Moreover, education, by its very nature presupposes the promotion and development of one's freedom, both of freedom of choice and of freedom of decision. Furthermore, the work of promoting freedom is an inescapable consequence of searching for universal truth in its integrity and totality. Now, the integrity of truth requires immunity from any restrictions in conducting the search for both objective and subjective truth,

---

[6] *De Veritate*, 2, 2c.
[7] *Summa contra Gentiles*, II, 81, 1625.
[8] *In II Analiticorum.*

and the totality of truth presupposes the creative dedication in cultivating all human values. In this sense one can read in the *Declaration on Christian Education*: "Surmounting hardship with a gallant and steady heart, they (students) should be helped to acquire gradually a more mature sense of responsibility toward ennobling their own lives through constant effort, and toward pursuing authentic freedom."[9] Education conceived as spiritual *metanoia*, tends towards fostering individual and personal self-mastery, in searching for the universal truth and all human values by promoting and developing one's authentic freedom.

III

However, if the distinctive mask of a catholic education consists in searching for the full development of spiritual life of man by transformation of his inner self, then the question arises: what is the fundamental task of catholic education, and how to reach a full synthesis of Christian principles and values in personal life of each and every faithful?

The proper resolution of the question what constitutes the catholic education depends, by necessity on the correct understanding of the very nature of the mission of the Catholic Church. On the occasion of the discussion on the "Scheme on the Catholic Church in the Modern World", the conciliar Fathers of Vatican II, debating on the original proposal "*Verbo et amore*", as the guiding principles for "fostering the human dignity,"[10] were searching for a more accurate expression for this fundamental role of the Church mission toward men. The then young Bishop of Kraków, Karol Wojtyla, suggested that

---

[9] "Declaration", *The Documents of Vatican II*, p. 639.

[10] *Acta Synodalia Sacrosancti Concilii Oecumenici Vaticana II*, v. III; pars VII (Rome: Typis Polyglottis Vaticanis, 1975), p. 381.

substituting the term *verbo* (word) with *veritas* (truth), would express the Christian teaching on human dignity more accurately. Although the discussed paragraph (20) of the original text has been abandoned, Wojtyla's expression has been included in the concluding words of paragraph 92 of *Gaudium et Spes*, as principles for "the unity and peace for the world at large."[11]

Indeed, truth and love are at the very core of Christ's Gospel as well as the teaching of His disciples. In fact, Christ identified Himself with those terms as the most appropriate characteristics of His entire mission. Answering to the question by Pilate as to whether He is a king, Jesus said: "Thou sayest it; I am a king. This is why I was born, and why I have come into the world, to bear witness to the truth. Everyone who is of the truth, hears my voice" (John 18:37). And when St. Thomas, one of His apostles, asked how one can know the truth, Christ said: "I am the way, and the truth, and the life" (John 14:6). In this existential response, our Lord indicated that He Himself to be the dynamic force which unites all people into one Family of Man: "You are my friends if you do the things I command you. No longer do I call you servants, because the servant does not know what his master does. But I have called you friends, because all things that I have heard from my Father I have made known to you. You have not chosen me, but I have chosen you, and have appointed you that you should go and bear fruit, and that your fruit should remain... These things I command you that you may love one another" (John 15:14-17). Commenting on St. John the Baptist testimony as to the mission of Christ, St. John said: "For the Law was given through Moses; grace and truth came through Jesus Christ" (John 1:17).

In view of these two principles, that is love and truth, which constitute the very nature of the Christian mission, the catholic education should consist of and be proclaimed, to use

---

[11] *The Documents of Vatican II*, p. 306.

the expression of Vatican II, "by witnessing to the truth and by hearing the truth (and to) extend(s) its dominion by the love."[12] However, in order to understand that truth and love are the fundamental principles of the Church's mission, we have to realize that the spiritual life of man takes place on two levels, namely, knowledge and action. The reason for this is that while our intellect directs itself toward truth, will tends to actualize the discovered truth in our personal life, thus realizing an existential integrity of the individual and personal harmony between mind and heart, knowing and feeling, namely cognition and action.

In order to achieve the existential integrity of an individual person by creating a harmonious synthesis between cognition and action, a catholic education should search for truth and love in that what they share in common, that is, in freedom. Referring to St. John (8:32): "you shall know the truth, and the truth shall make you free", Karol Wojtyla said to the conciliar Fathers: *"Non datur libertas sine veritate."*[13] Freedom so considered, is according to Wojtyla, not the end but the means and conditions for reaching the truth: *"Libertas . . . est propter veritatem."*[14] In his article "Zywotne tradycje uniwersytetu europejskiego" (The vital traditions of European university) Wojtyla strengthened his original statement by quoting from the "Declaration on Religious Freedom":

> It is in accordance with their dignity as persons - that is, beings endowed with reason and free will, and therefore privileged to bear personal responsibility - that all men should be at once impelled by nature and also bound by a moral obligation to seek the truth, especially religious truth. They are also bound to adhere to the truth, once it is known, and to order their whole life in accord with the demands of truth. However, men cannot discharge these obligations in a manner in keeping with their own

---

[12] *Ibid.*, p. 691.
[13] *Acta Synodalia*, v. III, pars 2, p. 531.
[14] *Ibid.*

nature, unless they enjoy immunity from external coercion as well as psychological freedom.[15]

In reaching truth man is also liberated by love, which touches upon the very depth of the inner-self of each individual. The catholic education then, should aim at attaining the objective truth which liberates man's subjective self from the blind forces of nature, and at searching for the highest values of human spirit. John Paul II said in this respect: "True academic freedom, must be seen in relation to the finality of the academic enterprise, which looks to the total truth of the human person."[16]

The liberating forces of truth and love result in man's creating cultural values, both on individual and social level of human life. The reason for this is that "striving for truth, as the foundation of human culture, remains in strict relationship with striving for good, with moral law and with a sensitivity for justice."[17] The cause of such a striving for truth and good springs from the natural ability of man to wonder. Cultivating the human spirit by developing the ability to wonder and to understand one's own inner and outer self requires that catholic education be based upon the principle of primacy of truth over pure *praxis*. John Paul II, in his address at the Catholic University of America, said: "The goals of Catholic higher education go beyond education for production, professional competence, technological and scientific competence; they aim at the ultimate destiny of the human person, at the full justice and holiness born of truth (cf. Eph. 4; 24)."[18] The authors of the "Declaration on Christian Eduction" are in this respect even more specific: "This sacred Synod strongly recommends that

---

[15] *Zeszyty Naukowe Katolickiego Uniwersytetu Lubelskiego*, 2 (1978), p. 52.

[16] *Pilgrim of Peace* (Washington, D.C.: Publication Office U.S. Catholic Conference, 1979), p. 167.

[17] "Kazanie na 600-lecie (UJ) w Kosciele Swietej Anny w Krakówie", *Tygodnik Powszechny*, 21 (1964).

[18] *Pilgrim of Peace*, p. 166.

Catholic colleges and universities and their faculties be conveniently located in diverse parts of the world, and that they be accorded the kind of support which will distinguish them for their academic pursuits rather than for the size of their enrollment..."[19]

The principle of the primacy of truth over pure *praxis* properly directs man toward the realization of his human nature as *persona*. In this context Karol Wojtyla proclaims that "the deepest and most essential factor in the conception of each catholic university" is "man, a human person with his proper tendency towards truth. This tendency is not only psychological but ontological one as well; this tendency which springs from (man's) rational nature. Here also originates the right to the truth and the obligation to search for it."[20] The primacy of truth over *praxis* will promote and find an "authentic freedom", for "truth serves liberty."[21] In conclusion our author says:

> In this area a catholic university is concerned with the task of education, since education consists of a proper subjugation of freedom - as man's power and right - to the truth. It is a deep opening of man towards his inner self, an immanent richness of his nature, from which it flows outward: towards other human beings."[22]

From this natural relationship between the inner and outer progress of the individual human person, based on the primacy of truth over pure *praxis*, and on the subordination of freedom to verity, Wojtyla postulates the principle of autonomy of things created by God, which is the very core of each and every catholic education: "In this light a university appears to us as an institution, where, in a certain manner, this rightful autono-

---

[19] The Documents of Vatican II, p. 649.
[20] "Uniwersytet Katolicki: koncepcja i zadania" (Na 50- lecie KUL), *Zeszyty Naukowe Katolickiego Uniwersytetu Lubelskiego*, 3-4 (1968), p. 14.
[21] *Ibid.*
[22] *Ibid.*

my is being worked out, and on which, to a great degree it depends. It is an autonomy gained through knowledge and truth. This autonomy expresses here also the fundamental and mature attitude of man toward the world; an attitude which conditions his domination over the world and, in a certain form, is already its domination."[23] The principle of the autonomy of things created by God, properly understood leads our author to establish a distinctive task for the catholic education:

> Among these tasks the highest priority should be given to research, that is to scientific study in its strictest sense. This endeavor gives to the whole community of teachers and students its basic characteristic trait - one could say - that of a university. Without it, teaching itself loses its proper depth, novelty and freshness. It is not the total sum of acquired information that makes a man well educated, but the ability of a creative penetration into a given topic - that, which is the condition of any research, its skill and method. Following the thoughts of the conciliar Constitution it could be said, that in this way only a university can be fully of service to this rightful autonomy of created things. The conveyance of knowledge alone, compared to this task, seems to be less important and secondary.[24]

The primacy of truth over pure *praxis* can, according to Wojtyla, also elucidate the object of our faith, i.e., God. As St. Thomas already stated "*Solus deus (est)...veritas per essentiam*". Also in this vein Wojtyla indicates that the very task of a catholic education consists of the "realization of the encounter of the knowledge of the Creator Himself and the creative cognition of man."[25] The same attitude was expressed in the "Letter of the Polish Episcopate on the Occasion of the 500th Anniversary of the Death of St. John of Kety." In this letter, co-signed by Cardinal Wojtyla and officially published in his archdiocese, we read:

---

23 *Ibid.*, p. 15.
24 *Ibid.*
25 *Ibid.*, p. 16.

> The long, over 80 years long life of the St. John of Kety, linked nearly in all its entirety with Kraków and the Jagiellonian University, was filled with the unceasing task of his professorship, vitalized to the very depth with love of God and fellow-men... His arduous scholarly work was permeated with constant thoughts on God. This great love of God animated his love of fellow-men and in particular, his love of students.[26]

The primacy of truth then, is also the primacy of God, and by the same token the main task of a Catholic University consists of the "intellectual apostolate."[27] This "intellectual apostolate," according to Wojtyla, means:

> to desire for other men, and even more, as effectively as possible, this truth, through which, basing on our own personal beliefs, we are witnesses to Christ; to desire it, respecting however, personal thinking and the free will of these men; to desire it, fully trusting in God's grace, which alone can make our desire fruitful. Apostolate then can exist only as a fruit of a profound spiritual life and inner culture of a Christian.[28]

IV

The basic role in the "intellectual apostolate belongs to philosophy and theology." In his address delivered at the Gregorian University John Paul II deeply stresses the need for studying the philosophy of being:

> I would like to say something specific at this point on philosophical studies in general, to which I am linked by long experience of teaching and research. In an ecclesiastical University, it is important that philosophy fulfill its traditional mandate, which is the methical investigation of the problems native to it and the research for their solution based on our ever valid philosophical

---

[26] "List Episkopatu na piecsetna rocznice smierci sw. Jana z Ket", *Tygodnik Powszechny*, 43 (1973).

[27] "Uniwersytet Katolicki", *Zeszyty Naukowe Katolickiego Uniwersytetu Lubelskiego*, p. 16.

[28] "Chrzescijanin a kultura", *Znak* 10 (1964), p. 1156.

patrimony, using the light of reason as its guide... But it is also important to notice that the relationship to our past patrimony ought not to be construed as a foreclosure of the possibility of a study which would endow modern and contemporary currents with value. What I said at the beginning of my pastoral ministry on the Chair of Peter was a cry to all not to fear to throw open the doors to Christ and bears repetition with regard to the great movements of contemporary thought, endowing with value their capacity for and inclination towards the whole truth.[29]

Philosophy, however, will be able "to open the doors for Christ", if it never becomes simply apologetics for the articles of our faith, and avoids - using the phrase of John Paul II from his address to the students from KUL - any "confessionalization".[30] In order to avoid the danger of "confessionalization" Cardinal Wojtyla warned us not to confuse act of faith with ideology, and not to understand evangelization of the Church as some type of indoctrination. Any "confessionalization" of philosophical investigation will inevitably lead to confusion of the philosophical truth with theological one, thus blurring reason and faith. Speaking on the goal of the catholic university John Paul II remarked:

> The goal of the university is knowledge and wisdom. The goal of the Church is salvation, the gospels, the order of love, and the supernatural order. These two orders were well distinguished by St. Thomas. They are not identical but they do supplement and support each other.[31]

Catholic philosophy, therefore, aims at an integration of truth in its totality. But, in order to achieve this, the integration of truth should be based on two principles:

---

[29] "Theology dynamically involved in prophetic mission of the Church," *L'Osservatore Romano*, January 21, 1980.

[30] Jan Pawel II, *Przemowienia, Homilie (Polska: 2, VI- 10, VI, 1979)* (Kraków: Znak, 1979), p. 159.

[31] *Ibid.*

1) the principle of the unity of truth, i.e., truth in one discipline should not contradict the other one, but to enforce the truth found in other fields of investigation;

2) the principle of methodological pluralism, i.e., in searching for truth one ought to attempt various approaches to reach truth in its manifold perspectives.

In short, Catholic philosophy respects the autonomy of particular disciplines, but expects mutual interdependency among various ways of searching for truth. Consequently, these two principles may become the guiding rules for any scholarly Catholic organization.

In *Optata totius* the conciliar Fathers of the Vatican II see the task for philosophy as cultivating a "solid and coherent understanding of man, of the world, and of God."[32] So understood, the purpose of philosophy in the Church is in complete agreement with John Paul II's *Sapientia Christiana,* where the present Pope encourages searching for a "living synthesis".[33] However, to achieve such a "living synthesis" catholic philosophy should be grounded upon:

1. "a philosophical heritage that is perennially valid;
2. "contemporary philosophical investigations" and
3. "the history of philosophy."[34]

So conceived, philosophy must be open to all the problematics of human reality, and one can find this kind of wisdom - according to John Paul II - in the perennial philosophy of *Doctor Angelicus*:

> The philosophy of St. Thomas deserved to be attentively studied and accepted with conviction by the youth of our day by reason of its spirit of openness and its universal characteristics which are hard to find in many trends of contemporary thought. What is

---

[32] *The Documents of Vatican II,* p. 450.
[33] *L'Osservatore Romano,* June 4, 1979.
[34] *Ibid.,* p. 8.

meant is an openness to the whole of reality in all its parts and dimensions, without either reducing reality or confining thought to particular forms or aspects (and without turning singular aspects into absolutes) as intelligence demands in the name of objective and integral truth about what is real. Such openness is also a significant and distinctive mark of the Christian faith, whose specific countermark is its catholicity. The basis and source of this openness lie in the fact that the philosophy of St. Thomas is a philosophy of being, that is, of the 'act of existing', whose transcendental value paves the most direct way to rise to the knowledge of subsisting being and pure act, namely, to God. On account of this, we can call this philosophy the philosophy of the proclamation of being, a chant in praise of what exists.[35]

The philosophy of St. Thomas provides us with a sound scientific methodology which enables the human intellect to find the ultimate truth of reality. As a matter of fact, St. Thomas derives his methodology from his philosophy of being.[36] In the words of John Paul II:

> It is also from this affirmation of being that the philosophy of St. Thomas draws its power to justify itself from the methodological point of view, as a branch of knowledge that cannot be reduced to any other science whatever, and as one that transcends them all by establishing itself as independent of them and at the same time as bringing them to completion in regard to their true nature.[37]

Methodology based on a proper philosophy of being "is able to, and indeed must, go beyond all that present itself directly in knowledge as an existing thing (given through experience) in order to reach 'that which subsists as sheer Existing' (*ipsum Esse subsistens*) and also creative Love."[38] Consequently, accepting metaphysics as a study of being *sub*

---

[35] "Perennial Philosophy of St. Thomas for the youth of our times", *L'Osservatore Romano*, December 17, 1979.

[36] Cf. St. Kaminski & M. Krapiec, *Z teorii i metodologii metafizyki* (Lublin: Towarzystwo Naukowe KUL, 1962).

[37] "Perennial philosophy", *L'Osservatore Romano*.

[38] *Ibid.*

ratione entis "St. Thomas pointed to that analogy which accompanies being as such, finding there the justification of the method for forming propositions dealing with the whole of reality and with the Absolute itself."[39]

Establishing the proper philosophical methodology in his search for the ultimate being, St. Thomas was able to lay the foundation for philosophical anthropology: "Insofar as methodology is concerned it would be hard to exaggerate the importance of this discovery for philosophical research, as indeed also for human knowledge."[40] In view of his philosophy

> St. Thomas is thinking of 'this' being and of this dignity when he speaks of man as that which is 'the most perfect thing in the whole nature' (*perfectissimum in tota natura*: S. Th. I, q. 29, a. 3), a 'person', requiring that it must be given exceptional and specific attention...[41]

The essential and distinctive mark of Aquinas's philosophy is the full development of both the spiritual and intellectual life of the entire man by discovering the truth about himself:

> There is still one more reason why the philosophy of St. Thomas has enduring value: its prevailing characteristic is that it is always in search of the truth. In his commentary on Aristotle, his favourite philosopher, he writes: 'Philosophy is not studied in order to find out what people may have thought but in order to discover what is true' (*De Coelo et Mundo*, I, lect. 22; ed. R. Spiazzi, n. 228).[42]

The discovered truth, however, St. Thomas enlightened by Christian principles and values:

> Man, St. Thomas points out, while he is *in statu viae*, can reach a certain understanding of the supernatural mysteries, thanks to

---

[39] *Ibid.*
[40] *Ibid.*
[41] *Ibid.*
[42] *Ibid.*

the use of his reason, but only to the extent to which the latter rests on the unshakable foundation of faith...[43]

In view of the enlightened truth by Christian faith "Christ is...the One who <u>made a radical change in the way of understanding life.</u> He shows that life is a passing over, not only to the limit of death, but to a new life. Thus the Cross became for us the supreme <u>Chair</u> of truth of God and of man."[44] Referring to *Gaudium et Spes* (n. 22) that Christ alone "reveals man fully to himself", John Paul II summarizes:

> St. Thomas has, moreover, shed the light of reason, purified and elevated by faith, on problems concerning man: on his nature as created to the image and likeness of God, on his personality as worthy of respect from the first moment of his conception, on his supernatural destiny as found in the beatific vision of God, One and Three. On this point we are indebted to St. Thomas for a precise and ever valid definition of that which constitutes man's essential greatness: 'he has charge of himself' (*ipse est sibi providens; Contra Gentiles*, III, 81).[45]

Notwithstanding the importance of philosophy, the greatest role in the evangelization belongs to the theological investigation. Theological investigation into faith under the guidance of the proper ecclesiastical authority is safeguarding "the Christian authenticity and unity of faith and moral teaching, in accordance with the injunction of the Apostle Paul: 'Proclaim the message and, welcome, or unwelcome, insist on it. Refute falsehood, correct error, call to obedience...' (2 Tim. 42)."[46] Theology ought to be under the control of the ecclesiastical control, because "it is the right of the faithful not to be troubled by theories and hypotheses that they are not expert in judging, or that are easily simplified or manipulated by public

---

[43] "Ideal ascent towards truth", *L'Osservatore Romano*, November 19, 1979.

[44] "Get to know Christ and make yourselves known to Him", *L'Osservatore Romano*, July 16, 1979.

[45] "Perennial philosophy", *L'Osservatore Romano*.

[46] "Historical bond between University and Church," *L'Osservatore Romano*, November 5, 1979, p. 5.

opinion for ends that are alien to the truth."47 Theologian, however, is free in his investigation, providing that he has "openness to the truth and the light comes from faith and from fidelity to the Church."48

The very nature of theology is to reflect upon the faith. But faith can be understood as a twofold act of believing, namely, an act of believing <u>that</u> which is nothing but an opinion, theory, and an act of believing <u>in</u> which consists in trusting and loving God. Having in mind this distinction, theologian must, while "penetrating all the riches of the divine plan as it reveals itself in human history and as one reflects on the magnificence of the cosmos,"49 attempt to reach the Christian wisdom. Referring to the Apostolic Constitution *Sapientia Christiana*, John Paul II writes:

> Christian wisdom, which the Church teaches by divine authority, continuously inspires the faithful of Christ to endeavour to relate human affairs and activities with religious values in a single living synthesis. Under the direction of these values all things are mutually connected for the glory of God and the integral development that includes both corporal and spiritual well-being.50

Summarizing, theology reflecting upon the mystery of faith understood as both an act of believing <u>that</u> and believing <u>in,</u> it is desiring "to pore over the depths of the revealed Word of God and the Church's living tradition with understanding and love."51 As a result of theological investigations will be "a thirst for human rights and justice, for morality and spirituality; a thirst for ultimate and definitive truths: a thirst for unity among Christians."52

---

47 *Ibid.*
48 *Ibid.*
49 "Theology dynamically involved", *L'Osservatore Romano*.
50 *Ibid.*
51 *Ibid.*
52 *Ibid.*

IV. THE ROLE OF CHRISTIAN CULTURE

The primary task of the apostolic action of the Church lies in cultivating the religious and moral life of individual persons. The religious-moral life cannot be separated from an individual's values, since it stems from all the values of a particular person. In cultivating religious-moral life then, the Catholic Church needs to be aware of and grant to man the right to personal views and occupation which support his own personal responsibilities and self-dependence. In the words of Karol Wojtyla:

> We are referring here not to a presence of Christianity in the works of culture in its material, but in its formal content, namely in its style or mode. We are referring to the Christian standard of the very act of creating, which obviously admits of countless variants and individualisms. Indeed, the Christian culture as found in the innermost core of each particular person is, in a way,

different and unique.[1]

In his pastoral action, the Church affects individuals in various ways by influencing their socio-cultural life. Historically it is possible to distinguish in the Christianization of a given society two types of action: 1. transforming an entire indigenous system of values and adapting it to the requirements of the catholic religion; 2. incorporating the precepts of the catholic religion into the collective cultural values.

These two types of apostolic action cannot be divided or separated in a concrete social situation of course, since in real life these two actions are interwoven and complement each other. This is a result of man's very nature as an individual and from the fact that, living in time and space, he is an environmental creature.

Christianization is a very complex and prolonged process. In evaluating the religious needs of a given society, the whole system of its present cultural values needs to be taken into consideration. Only from this wider perspective can the Church in a particular society apply appropriate methods of action or establish suitable tasks and goals.

In order to establish a proper approach in these matters, it is also imperative to understand the role of Christ's Church on earth and her duty towards each and every man.

I

In human nature one can distinguish both stable and changeable characteristics. From the stable elements, man derives autonomy, spirituality; the changeable elements permit man to be the subject and creator of history. The complex nature of these elements is the source of a constant tension between man's

---

[1] "Chrzescijanin a kultura", *Znak* 10 (1964), p. 1155.

desire for preservation of the familiar and yearning for new developments. In the spiritual order of man, as expressed by Wojtyla, new civilizations and new cultures can be traced to that tension, thus constituting man's very existence on the earth:

> Every man, in a certain way lives by culture, and remains in the orbit of a culture of his contemporary time. In a certain sense, the greatest result of culture is man himself--not his works or products as such--but his very self. Man's action and its fruits remain in a strict relation to what man is, and by what he lives. Thus the works of man's culture are nothing else but the fruit of that product of culture which is man himself.[2]

The basic element in forming a civilization or culture is the environment within which an individual or a particular social group lives.[3] According to the Danish anthropologist, Kaj Birket-Smith, culture is merely an expression of the way man adapts to nature, civilization is his victory over it, often gained in spite of unfavorable conditions of natural environment.[4] The decisive element in the emergence of man's cultural and civilizational life is man's attitude towards his natural and human environment.

Within the natural environment man first of all strives to assure his dominance over all nature in order to establish a permanent place of residence. The instinct of self-preservation demands safety and security. But in striving to dominate his external environment, man attempts to take command of nature, transforming the natural environment into a human one. Consequently, his attitude toward nature undergoes both a unification and a diversification. Man establishes various types and modes of social life.

---

[2] *Ibid.*, p. 1154.
[3] Cf. A.L. Kroeber and Clyde Kluckhom, *Culture* (New York: Random House, 1952).
[4] *Primitive Man and his Ways* (London: Oldhams Press Ltd., Long Acre, 1960).

The development of man's life on earth can be characterized by a rhythmic transgressing the state of adaptation to an environment into that of domination over it. Arnold Toynbee conceives the civilizational and cultural life of man as a rhythm of "challenge" and "response"; the challenge of the external conditions and the response given by a particular society.[5] In cases where the external environment does not provide sufficient safety, and the challenge for mastering it are beyond the possibilities of a given social group, man is forced either to change the place of his residence or to seek different methods of adaptation and a new way of living. In the first case, migration takes place, in the other, new forms of adaptation are conducive either to development and progress, or to the decline and downfall of a particular social grouping.

Recognizing that adaptation and migration are not only two essential facts in the history of humanity but are also the basic elements in the development of the civilizational and cultural life of man, is of great importance. It allows a proper understanding of the cycle of the emergence and downfall of human societies in the past as well as the present. Depending on the relationship between the process of adaptation and migration and their inter-connection, different kinds of societies will develop.

Christianity plays an exceptional role in perfecting the spiritual life of man. Catholic religion is described by the historians of civilization and the philosophers of history as dynamic and open.[6] In his address to the NCCB of West Germany, held in Cologne in September 1978, Wojtyla made the following remarks: "The concern about culture, concern about an exchange in this field belongs to the tasks of the Church; it

---

[5] *A Study of History*, VI (London: Oxford University Press, 1939), p. 324.
[6] Cf. Henri Bergson, *Les deux sources de la morale et de la religion*, ed. III-]me (Paris: Alcan, 1932).

rests also in the orbit of our ecclesiastical service of a bishop."[7] Indeed, it would be most difficult to find any stronger statement on the task of cultural values in the role of apostolic activity of the Church. The reason for stressing the cultural values in the religious life of the faithful stems from the fact that culture itself is, according to Karol Wojtyla:

> ...one of those terms which are most intimately connected with man, and which define his existence, and in a sense point to his very essence. Man makes culture, needs culture, and through culture creates himself. Culture consists of a set of facts, through which man expresses himself more than through anything else. He expresses himself to himself and to others. All works of culture which last longer than man's life are witnesses to him. It is a testimony to spiritual life, and to the human spirit which lives not only on the account of mastering all matter, but lives in itself by ideals accessible to him alone, and only for him meaningful. He lives through truth, goodness and beauty--and outwardly expresses its own spiritual life and objectivizes it in his deeds. Man then, as a maker of culture gives witness to the very humanness.[8]

In evaluating the Christian religion and its place in the formation of civilization and culture, however, one ought to be aware of the fact that in reality there never was (nor can it be) a universal and never-changing Christian concept of the ideal social life. In other words, there cannot exist in Christian doctrine any specific or ideal vision of the world or of a social entity. To expect the opposite leads to ontological heresy, according to which, that which is particular in the realm of human life can be limited to that which is general and universally bound forever, and therefore what is particular would, in fact, be that which is general and can be expressed in norms. The realization of the fact that there is no adequate and exclusive vision of Christian reality, and that there cannot be one, is of utmost importance, since it also implies that there is no

---

[7] *Tygodnik Powszechny*, 44 (1978).
[8] "Chrzescijanin a kultura", *Znak*.

specifically Christian culture, civilization, state, politics, economy, party.

In the history of the world and of contemporary culture, no particular social group (including the Church) can claim to be the adequate Christian realization of the precepts of faith and morality, nor that it provides a full solution to a given historical situation. In any situation, there can be various possibilities of appropriate reactions and styles. To make a <u>choice</u> from among the different possibilities is of utmost personal significance for a given individual or particular social group.

The influence of Christianity on the spiritual life of man is diversified and depends on historical conditions. The historical solution of a particular problem by a Christian, and the resolution of a spiritual conflict, is connected with a certain risk and responsibility. Every Christian faces many possibilities for action and in making choices needs to find Christian guidelines. Today's world is a pluralistic world, also making the discovery of such guidelines difficult.

The pluralism of contemporary society bears consequences for all Christians in the formation of attitudes towards the social reality in which they live. Diversification of our present life makes us aware of two facts: 1. Christians, as such, do not have an infallible, ready-made program to guide the establishment of a state, culture, economy, etc.; 2. the Church cannot be considered as the only and immediate object in developing all inner-worldly possibilities.

Of course, a situation can arise which will demand a united response from all Christians. But we cannot consider any uniform historically conditioned action as the only just one. We cannot postulate that the Christian norms provide the only defined and valid ways for resolving the dilemma of multiple possibilities. Christians ought to free themselves from confusing principles and their attempts at seeking solutions in the historical and cultural conditions of any given era which already belongs to the past.

Instead, the world awaits proper concrete applications of Christ's message to given historical situations. Christians, endowed as they are with a historical mission, ought to have the courage to present these proposals. They cannot, however, propagate them in the name of Christianity. Within this can be found the reason why the Church has to retreat from politics, or rather modify its political demands. It is neither opportunism nor resignation from proclaiming Christian principles. It stems from a sense of awareness of Christianity as defined, transcendent lifestyles. The preservation of this awareness will free the Church from the responsibility for historical reactions.

The variety of possibilities opening up before any historically-centered man demands the existence of a subject by which they would be confronted. The proper subject, according to Rahner, is either the state or an internationally organized association of nations. The state acquires specific importance and plays a fundamental role in forming a vision of the contemporary world. The state as a component in the life of a given society and in the life of an individual as well, increases more and more, enfolding ever bigger sectors and areas of human life.[9]

The solicitude of the Church for the spiritual well- being of people is not limited to moral and religious affairs, but enfolds all the areas of their social and cultural life too, because the latter are basic elements of life in human existence. In "Pastoral Constitution on the Church in the Modern World" we read:

> Various conditions of community living, as well as various patterns for organizing the goods of life, arise from diverse ways of using things, of laboring, of expressing oneself, of practicing religion, of forming customs, of establishing laws and juridical

---

[9] Karl Rahner, *Sendung und Gnade* (Innsbruck: Tyrolia Verlag, 1959).

institutions, of advancing the arts and sciences, and of promoting beauty. Thus the customs handed down to it form for each human community its proper patrimony. Thus, too, is fashioned the specific historical environment which enfolds the men of every nation and age and from which they draw the values which permit them to promote human and civic culture.[10]

Consequently, in line with this understanding of the cultural life, the Church proclaims the right of all men to respect and develop their own cultural traditions the way they see fit. In this vein Wojtyla concludes:

> This participation consists of strictly personal acts derived from man's spiritual life; acts, which simultaneously build also the Church as a cohesive and mature community. Having still quite vividly in mind the discussions on Church which took place during the second session of the Council, I would like to elaborate on these acts. First of all then, every Christian is a confessor of his faith. He gives witness to God's truth as revealed by and in Christ, and to his own beliefs in this truth. Witnessing does not denote a separate sphere of action, but searches for a place for itself in all men. It remains in strict contact with creating culture in its deepest and most inner meaning, where its object is simply man himself. But in consequence of confessing or in witnessing Christ as the inner feature of man, it passes through into the object of culture created by man. This process of passing through into the objects made by man is unavoidable and achieved both subtly and openly. It is perhaps the best attestation to the inner Christian culture of man. In any case, the presence of Christianity in the acts of culture takes there its very source.[11]

II

The basic concern of the Church for the problematics of cultural life is in her apostolic and missionary activity. This twofold

---

[10] *The Documents of Vatican II*, ed. Walter Abbott (New York: Guild Press, 1966), pp. 259-260.

[11] "Chrzescijanin a kultura", *Znak*, p. 1155.

characteristic of the activities of the Church lies in the fulfillment of the religio-spiritual mission among people. This understanding of the apostolic and missionary legacy is based on Christian universalism, which, regarding the missionary pastorate, demands consideration for all spiritual values of each individual person. In this vein Wojtyla also writes:

> Men who create Christian culture and are consciously engaged in its renewal in contemporary terms, ought to thoroughly rethink the truth about the Church; the truth which became the main concern of the Second Vatican Council. It is this truth in which all the actions directed towards a renewal of catholicism (*accomodata renovatio*) and unification of all Christians find their base and common plateau. Essentially, the truth about the Church is a truth through which every Christian can find himself in all his fullness. There is a profound correlation between the beingness of Church as a Mystical Body of Christ and the People of God, and the beingness of every singular Christian, lay or religious. Every one of us is personally a Christian through participation in the larger community of Church.[12]

The apostolic and missionary characteristics of the Church cannot conflict with one another. Any apparent differences result from the way they are being understood by the faithful. Commenting on the teaching of Vatican II on the apostolic and missionary activity of the Church, Wojtyla observes:

> Ensuing from this very important element of our participation in the Church and in culture is another one, which the Vatican Council stressed in an unprecedented fashion, namely apostolate and mission. To confess one's faith is to give witness to Christ before others and to be an apostle means to be conscious of that mission to which man is called on the basis of his witnessing, and to accept full responsibility for it. Apostolate denotes also a particular form of mature experiencing the act of faith. To be an apostle means to desire for other men, and even more, as effectively as possible, this truth through which, basing on our own personal beliefs, we are witnesses to Christ; to desire it, respecting however, personal thinking and the free will of these

---

[12] *Ibid.*

men; to desire it, fully trusting in God's grace, which alone can make our desire fruitful. Apostolate then can exist only as a fruit of a profound spiritual life and inner culture of a Christian.[13]

Thus, in the process of historical development, different visions of the Divine Kingdom on earth emerge, depending on the given era in which the Catholic Church lives and acts. The tension between the apostolic and missionary activity of Christ's Church is permanent, and evident from the very beginning of the Christian religion.

At the onset of Christianity, the missionary activity of the Church was, of necessity, primarily stressed. This led to decentralization of administration. One can deduce this fact from the letters of St. Paul addressed to the particular community in Corinth, Ephesus and Rome, as well as to individual persons, Timothy, Titus, or Philemon. The vision of the Church as particular communities of converted pagans stemmed from Christ's commandment: "Go, then, to all peoples everywhere and make them my disciples: baptize them in the name of the Father and of the Son and of the Holy Spirit, and teach them to obey everything I have commanded you" (Matt. 28:19). Conversely, the universalism of particular churches is based on a perception of the unity of diverse peoples, joined by faith in Christ's mission, independent from their origin, race, or nationality.

The tendency toward centralization among the first followers of Christ originated from converted Jews, who attempted to unify Christianity with the idea of Jewish messianism. Eventually, a tension arose between the tendency to "Jewishize" Christianity and the tendency to dominate over the Jewishness of the converted by underscoring the universality of the Church. St. Paul, stressing particularism, aimed at making the Christian religion a wholeness, independent from any particular nationality or any religious tendencies, thereby proving himself to be an adherent of the decentral-

---

[13] *Ibid.*, pp. 1155-1156.

ization of Church authorities. St. Paul limited his apostolic activity to areas not yet reached by any other apostle or disciple of Christ. St. Peter, on the other hand, under the influence of converted Jews, stressed the apostolic character of the Church, and consequently aimed at centralizing all the faithful through their judaization. From the perspective of historical development we know that Paul's idea eventually dominated and that even the Prince of the Apostles became convinced of the universal character of Christ's message. One could posit that the translocation of the center of Christianity from Jerusalem to Rome was actually an attempt to make the Church independent from Judaism, and a re-directing of apostolic activity towards the entire world, unified in the ideal of the universality of the dying Roman Empire.

The ultimate division of the Roman Empire caused the emergence of two centers of Christianity, namely, one in the East, and one in the West. And the tension between the tendency of Rome to centralize based on the apostolic mission of the Church was contrasted to the Byzantine drive toward decentralization in the name of the missionary character of the Church as composed of particular local churches. Medieval Christianity faced an ideological conflict in the division of Christ's Church between the Rome papacy and the patriarchy of Byzantium. Naturally, over the decades further differentiation and divisions have taken place on both sides. On the threshold of modern times, reformers began to underline the Christian missionary idea and the particularism of individual communities by the Reformed Church. The tendencies of the Reformed Church went as far as to subjugate the church authorities to secular authorities, following the principle of *"cuius regio, eius religio"*. In answering the protestant tendencies toward decentralization, the Catholic Church turned to stressing the apostolic character of the Church in its hierarchic structure, and through that, the centralism of the Church authorities personified by the successor of St. Peter.

Consequently, in the last century a new tension in the Catholic Church was to be observed; this time between the idea of papal primacy as opposed to the collegiality of the entire faithful in the Church. The Council of Trident formulated the essence of the Church as a community of faithful remaining under the authority of the Pope. This concept predominated and was only overcome by the Second Vatican Council, when the Church was redefined as the universal sacrament of salvation, encompassing all men of good will, regardless of their origin or denomination; only malevolent atheists were exempted from participation in the Church.

The vision of the Church as defined by the last Vatican Council revived the idea of unity and brought to the awareness of the faithful fundamental differences in understanding the proper role of the Catholic Church in a contemporary world. The adherents of decentralization accuse the Apostolic See of institutionalism and legalism in matters of morality and faith, as well as formalistic rigidity in social issues. The defenders of central authority charge their opponents with faithlessness to the Christian teaching of unity and disrespect of the Pope's authority. They attempt to re-subjugate the post-Vatican II Church to the old principles and rules of ecclesiastic discipline. In this critical situation, Wojtyla admonishes:

> The creative action of Christian culture can be both confession of faith or witnessing, and an apostolic vocation. It is exactly for this reason that we ought to rethink under which conditions we are free effectively to desire for others their participation in the same truth, in which, due to Christ and the Church, we are called to share. Truth is the foundation of culture--and we must, with the utmost care, safeguard and protect this foundation.[14]

The presence of Christianity in the cultural life of man, however, is not static but dynamic, because the need for proclaiming the Good News to all nations of all times requires a constant accommodation and renewal of the apostolic and

---

[14] *Ibid.*, p. 1156.

missionary activity of the Church. It also demands that all spiritual values of the individual person be taken into consideration. However, the dynamic character of Christian religion points to the creative attitude of the Church towards the cultural values of all people who live in different times and in various milieus. Therefore, in her apostolic activity the church must adapt different attitudes in order to respond to the constant changes and development of spiritual needs taking place in various historical epochs. The apostolic and missionary activity of the Church, then, must of necessity be universal in order to fulfill the needs of all men. The proper subject of spiritual and cultural life, therefore, is man living in a particular time. In the Pastoral "Constitution on the Church in the Modern World" we read:

> Living in various circumstances during the course of time, the Church, too, has used in her preaching the discoveries of different cultures to spread and explain the message of Christ to all nations, to probe it and more and more deeply understand it, and to give it better expression in liturgical celebrations and in the life of the diversified community of the faithful. But, at the same time, this Church, sent to all peoples of every time and place, is not bound exclusively and indissolubly to any race or nation, nor to any particular way of life or customary pattern of living, ancient or recent. Faithful to her own tradition and, at the same time conscious of her universal mission, she can enter into communion with various cultural modes, to her own enrichment and theirs too.[15]

By involving herself in the cultural life of the faithful, the Church attempts not only to create a favorable environment for preaching the Gospel but for the education of the whole man. In the education of the whole man, the Church, by the same token, also contributes in the development of a given culture. In this respect the Fathers of the Vatican II Council write:

> The Church recalls to the mind of all that culture must be made to bear on the integral perfection of the human person, and on

---

[15] *The Documents of Vatican II*, p. 264.

the good of the community and the whole of society. Therefore the human spirit must be cultivated in such a way that there results a growth in its ability to wonder, to understand, to contemplate, to make personal judgments, and to develop a religious, moral, and social sense[16].

III

While the Church highly praises the value of culture and has concern for its development it is also deeply concerned with the contemporary spiritual crisis of man. Referring to St. Paul who says that "all creation groans and travails in pain until now" (Rom. 8:22), John Paul II asks: "Does not the previously unknown immense progress--which has taken place in the course of this century--in the field of man's dominion over the world itself--reveal, to a previously unknown degree, that manifold subjection 'to futility'?" And he immediately answers:

> It is enough to recall certain phenomena, such as the threat of pollution of the natural environment in areas of rapid industrialization, or of the armed conflicts continually breaking out over and over again, or the prospectives of self- destruction through the use of atomic, hydrogen, neutron and similar weapons, or the lack of respect for the life of the unborn. The world of the new age, the world of space flights, the world of the previously unattained conquests of science and technology--is it not also the world "groaning in travail" that "waits with eager longing for the revealing of the sons of God" (II, 8).[17]

How should this paradoxical situation of contemporary man be resolved? Why is there such a tension between the actual need of man for cultural life and the factual abasement of his dignity in contemporary life? John Paul II answers: "It is the drama of man who is deprived of an essential dimension of

---

[16] *Ibid.*, p. 265.
[17] "Redemptor Hominis", *Acta Apostolicae Sedis* 71 (1979).

his being, namely his search for the infinite" (II, 9).[18] But, since the essential need for infinity in man has been given by the fact of the Incarnation, human dignity for man consists in Jesus Christ. Moreover, by Incarnation Christ became "the center of the universe and of history, restoring for man the original God's loving plan":

> God entered the history of humanity and, as a man, became an actor in that history, one of the thousands of millions of human beings but at the same time unique! Through the Incarnation, God gave human life the dimension that he intended man to have from his first beginning: he has granted that dimension definitively--in the way that is peculiar to him alone, in keeping with his eternal love and mercy, with the full freedom of God--and he has granted it also with the bounty that enables us, in considering the original sin and the whole history of the sins of humanity, and in considering the errors of the human intellect, will and heart, to repeat with amazement the words of the sacred liturgy: "O happy fault...which gained us so great a redeemer!" (I, 1).[19]

Christ, then, is the fundamental source of the restoration of human dignity and the ultimate power for renewal of human existence on earth both in man's individual and communal life. Seeking to restore God's original plan, Christ as man's Redeemer, calls him to be a witness to the Lord and to be his apostle of the Good News. Thus he seeks to participate in the redemption of the entire world. The depth of such a vocation of any Christian is rooted in his heart which "compels man to be 'for others', to have a generous relationship with others... Without relationship and without self-giving, the whole of human existence loses its meaning."[20]

The contemporary crisis of man consists precisely in the absence of the spirit of self-giving, and the refusal to accept

---

[18] *Ibid.*
[19] *Ibid.*
[20] Karol Wojtyla, *Sign of Contradiction* (New York: The Seabury Press, 1979), p. 132.

Christ as the best example of 'being-for-others' (to use a Sartrean expression). Today's man is a witness not only of the process of the degradation of his dignity, but also to the imminent danger of his annihilation. In the words of John Paul II:

> The man of today seems ever to be under threat from what he produces, that is to say from the result of the work of his hands and, even more so, of the work of his intellect and the tendencies of his will. All too soon, and often in an unforeseeable way, what this manifold activity of man yields is not only subjected to "alienation," in the sense that it is simply taken away from the person who produces it, but rather it turns against man himself, at least in part, through the indirect consequences of its effects returning on himself. It is or can be directed against him. This seems to make up the main chapter of the drama of present-day human existence in its broadest and universal dimension. Man therefore lives increasingly in fear. He is afraid that what he produces--not all of it, of course, or even most of it, but part of it and precisely that part that contains a special share of his genius and initiative--can radically turn against himself; he is afraid that it can become the means and instrument for an unimaginable self- destruction, compared with which all the cataclysms and catastrophes of world history known to us seem to fade away. (III, 15).[21]

The question arises: What is the chief cause of the danger of man's 'self-destruction'? The answer seems to be obvious: contemporary man has lost the balance between the outer progress and the inner self-conquest. As a result of his fascination with the enormous technological progress, man now neglects his spirituality. Heidegger warns us:

> Man in his being is menaced by the conviction, that the technical development will dominate the order of the world; and this domination reduces all *'ordo'*.... The world is losing the possibility of salvation. Not only sanctity, that was the road to God, is lost, but even the access to sanctity, i.e., the very notion of sanctity must be laid aside.[22]

---

[21] "Redemptor Hominis", *Acta Apostolicae Sedis*.
[22] *Holzwege* (Frankfurt A.M.: Niemeyer, 1950), p. 272.

In spite of this utterly pessimistic warning, contemporary man must try to overcome the danger of 'self-destruction' and to try to return to Christ and to preserve peace by all means.

In his Message for the XX World Day of Peace (January 1, 1987) John Paul II asks:

> Can true peace exist when men, women and children cannot live in full human dignity? Can there be a lasting peace in a world ruled by relations-- social, economic and political--that favor one group or nation at the expense of another? Can genuine peace be established without an effective recognition of that wonderful truth that we are all equal in dignity, equal because we have been formed in the image of God who is our Father?[23]

The answer to these questions of the Pontiff is positive, and in his view there are two solutions to universal peace: development and solidarity. These two solutions to universal peace are based on the obvious fact that "we are one human family."[24] By having the same nature and having been created by the same God, men of different races, various cultures and divergent histories, should seek peaceful co-existence.

In establishing a properly understood development and solidarity among people, we must seek to overcome the obstacles which are dividing the members of one Family of Man. In order to achieve solidarity among men, we must restore "the fundamental equality and the dignity of man."[25]

John Paul II holds that there are three main obstacles to establishing the solidarity:

> a *xenophobia* that closes nations in on themselves or which leads governments to enact discriminatory laws against people in their own countries;
>
> the closing of borders in an arbitrary and unjustifiable way so that

---

[23] "Development and solidarity: two keys to peace", *L'Osservatore Romano*, 22-29 December 1986.
[24] *Ibid.*
[25] *Ibid.*

people are effectively deprived of the ability to move and to better their lot, to be reunited with their loved ones, or simply to visit their family or reach out in care and understanding to others;

<u>ideologies</u> that preach hatred or distrust, systems that set up artificial barriers. Racial hatred, religious intolerance, class divisions are all too present in many societies, both openly and covertly. When political leaders erect such divisions into internal systems or into policies regarding relationships with other nations, then these prejudices strike at the core of human dignity. They become a powerful source of counteractions that further foster division, enmity, repression and warfare. Another evil, which in this past year brought so much suffering to people and havoc to society, is terrorism.[26]

To overcome these three obstacles which are causing hatred among men, we must "build open and honest relationships among peoples;" we must build alliances between nations, in order to foster cooperation among individuals and particular groups.[27] In order to achieve such a peaceful co-existence, we must develop "a spirit that is open to dialogue."[28] The spirit of dialogue must be based on truth which "seeks to build up rather than destroy, to unite rather than divide."[29] The spirit of dialogue based on truth should bring social justice in the area of development. In applying the spirit of solidarity to the social development of the world, John Paul II writes:

When we reflect on commitment to solidarity in the field of development, the first and most basic truth is that development is a question of people. People are the subjects of true development, and the aim of true development is people. The integral development of people is the goal and measure of all development projects. That all people are at the centre of development is a consequence of the oneness of the human family; and this is irrespective of any technological or scientific discoveries that the future may hold. People must be the focus of all that is

---

[26] *Ibid.*
[27] *Ibid.*
[28] *Ibid.*
[29] *Ibid.*

done to improve the conditions of life. People must be active agents, not passive recipients, in any true development process.[30]

By respecting the principle of equality of all men, human development will "promote values that truly benefit individual and society."[31] The spirit of solidarity which promotes human and personal values will foster integral development which will

> protect and defend the legitimate freedom of every person and the rightful security of every nation. Without this freedom and security, the very conditions for development are missing. Not only individuals but also nations must be able to share in the choices which affect them. The freedom that nations must have to ensure their growth and development as equal partners in the family of nations is dependent on the reciprocal respect among them. Seeking economic, military or political superiority at the expense of the rights of other nations places in jeopardy any prospects for true development or true peace.[32]

The personalistic principle which recognizes in each and every person a unique and unrepeatable dignity, will lead all men to unity:

> To recognize the social solidarity of the human family brings with it the responsibility to build on what makes us one. This means promoting effectively and without exception the equal dignity of all as human beings endowed with certain fundamental and inalienable human rights. This touches all aspects of our individual life, as well as our life in the family, in the community in which we live, and in the world. Once we truly grasp that we are brothers and sisters in a common humanity, then we can shape our attitudes towards life in the light of the solidarity which makes us one. This is especially true in all that relates to the basic universal project: peace.[33]

In conclusion peace is possible if we will follow the spirit of

---

[30] *Ibid.*
[31] *Ibid.*
[32] *Ibid.*
[33] *Ibid.*

solidarity based on the truth of equality of our nature as human persons, and the spirit of mutual help in developing our natural and human resources. Summarizing his proposal for the preservation of peace on earth, John Paul II writes:

> <u>Solidarity is ethical</u> in nature because it involves an <u>affirmation of value</u> about humanity. For this reason, its implications for human life on this planet and for international relations are also ethical: our common bonds of humanity demand that we live in harmony and that we promote what is good for one another. These ethical implications are the reason why <u>solidarity is a basic key to peace.</u> In this same light, <u>development</u> takes on its full meaning. It is no longer a question merely of improving certain situations or economic conditions. Development ultimately becomes a question of <u>peace,</u> because it helps to achieve what is good for others and for the human community as a whole.[34]

---

[34] *Ilbid.*

V. THE CATHOLIC CHURCH AND THE ECUMENICAL MOVEMENT

Karol Wojtyla's interest in the ecumenical movement began when he was appointed bishop in the Archdiocese of Kraków. Almost yearly started in 1963, the newly appointed ordinary delivered a special homily in the Basilica of the Dominicans in Kraków on January 25th, the feast of the conversion of St. Paul. In his first sermon on ecumenism Wojtyla defined it as "a conversion toward unity of all Christians."[1] We find the same teaching 15 years later when Cardinal Wojtyla became John Paul II: "...the eagerness to put an end to the intolerable scandal of Christian divisions, means that we must avoid all

---

[1] *Kazania 1962-1978* (Kraków: *Znak*, 1979), p. 354.

superficiality, all rash enthusiasms which might hinder the progress towards unity."[2]

But the question arises: what stimulated such intense interest concerning the ecumenical movement in the then young ordinary of Kraków? Such a question is justified, particularly when we realize that Poland is predominantly a Catholic country.

It is a fact, however, that several Christian communities belonging to a variety of religious denominations exist in Poland. In 1966 the following Christian churches existed in Poland: Autocephalous Orthodox Church (500,000), Evangelical Augsburg Confession (100,000), Evangelical Reformed Church (5,000), Methodist Church (6,000), Polish Baptist Church (2,500), Polish National Church (32,200) and Old Catholic Church (25,000).[3] All these denominations are organized into the Polish Ecumenical Council which has been in existence since 1945 (only the Adventists and Jehovah's Witnesses do not belong to this council, but they number not more than about 20,000).[4]

So far as the Roman Catholic Church in Poland is concerned, the late Cardinal Stefan Wyszynski initiated ecumenical awareness among the faithful, first in his diocese at Warsaw, and then by organizing a permanent Ecumenical Commission at the Polish NCCB. In the statutes of the Ecumenical Commission we read:

> The purpose of the Ecumenical Commission is to conduct the works which are oriented toward the unification of believers in Christ the Lord, and especially to bring to life the decree "*De Oecumenismo*" and other directives of the Holy See and of the Polish NCCB which pertain to the development of the ecumeni-

---

[2] *Through the Year with John Paul II*, Tony Castle, ed. (New York: Crossroad, 1981), p. 28.

[3] Cf. Jan Kloczowski, "Czy ekumenizm w Polsce jest aktualny," *Tygodnik Powszechny*, 3 (1970).

[4] Jan Karcz, "Polski ruch ekumeniczny," *Hejnal Mariacki*, 2 (1969), pp. 4-5.

cal movement in Poland-- organizing researches with regard to the problems of ecumenism and shaping the ecumenical consciousness among the clergy and faithful in Poland--attempting to bring into close contact the Catholic Church and separated brothers. In realizing the above purposes the Ecumenical Council uses all reachable means and especially:-- It organizes all different and various Ecumenical Council conferences and matters, preparing ceremonies, retreats and other pastorate ecumenical actions on the national level--it cooperates with diocesan Ecumenical Council centers--it maintains contact and prepares Ecumenical Council dialogues with separated brothers in the country and abroad.[5]

The basic aim of the Polish ecumenical movement consists, then, in the "formation of an ecumenical consciousness" among the Catholic faithful in Poland. But one can still ask: what are the reasons for developing an ecumenical consciousness in a country which is predominantly Catholic? Cardinal Wojtyla points to two reasons, namely, the historical heritage of the Polish experience in the development of the ecumenical movement in the past, both on the national and international levels, and the constant need to defend Poland's national identity.

From the very beginning Poland found herself at the crossroads of two cultural and racial centers; she is the last country of the West and the first country of the East. Moreover, Poland's geopolitical position in Europe points out her role in the sphere of sociopolitical and cultural- religious life. In the words of Karol Wojtyla:

> We Poles remain in overwhelming majority Catholic, finding in Catholicism, in the Catholic Church, the spiritual position of defending ourselves against our partitioners from the East who represent the Orthodox Church and those from the West who represent Protestantism, preserving, however--I would like to stress in our Catholicism, in the Catholic Church--some type of inner thanks for our identity and our spiritual steadfastness, due to which our nation survived, respecting however, at the same

---

[5] *Ibid.*, p. 4.

time, the convictions of others.[6]

Poland's appearance as a Christian state and Catholic nation in the 10th century meant, first, the entrance of the Slavic race into European civilization and, as such, an end to the exclusive German influence in shaping the face of future Europe; second, the actual spread of Latin civilization east of the Elb along with the movement of Slavic cultural elements into the West. Thus, from the very beginning Poland became a bridge between the East and the West. In such a situation, the only solution was to search for coexistence. Commenting on the Polish past, Cardinal Wojtyla writes:

> As it is known, our country, in her millennium, was a place for co-living, co-existing and co-operation of Christians of various denominations and churches. This has been especially true since the fifteenth and sixteenth centuries. Certainly, from the Jagiellonian period the history of this co-living and co-operation, of this co-existence has had its own shadows but it surely has had its bright spots. Poland was never the stage for religious wars. During the many disputes, sometimes very fiery, with a variety of positions, Poles always preserved peace in this respect. This came from the same roots from which Council Vatican II has now introduced contemporary ecumenical positions, especially with respect to religious liberty and the spiritual freedom of man, namely: respect of human freedom. We Poles have always--it might be the case that we are too proud in this respect and we therefore falsely evaluate this--but it seems we have always had a great love for freedom; we have the understanding of truth that each man has his own dignity. This dignity is bound with his consciousness, with his conscience, with his freedom.[7]

To understand better Wojtyla's teaching on ecumenical consciousness, it would be helpful to point to certain historical facts, especially since Wojtyla quite frequently refers to Polish ecumenical experience of the past.

---

[6] Kazania, p. 398.

• THE CHURCH AND THE ECUMENICAL MOVEMENT •

II

The greatest advantage Poland gained from her baptism in the Latin Rite was the consolidation of the entire society into one state and the birth of a new style of c ultural life. Culture is one of the basic sources from which the spirit of a nation springs. In the words of Wojtyla: "Culture is a testimony to (man's) spiritual life and to the human spirit, which lives not only because it has mastery over all matter, but because it lives in itself by ideals accessible to man alone."[8] The most characteristic of Poland's cultural achievements in the course of her 1,000 years of existence is the spirit of oneness and freedom.

From the very beginning of her existence Poland was never a homogeneous social entity. Polish society always represented an unusual mosaic of different races, nationalities and tribes. The well-known German psychologist Ernest Kretschmer pointed out that in Poland the Slavic races met the Asiatic ones. On the other hand, according to Czekanowski's findings, through the center of Poland runs the largest belt of Nordic races in all Europe. In the territory of Poland one can also find Tartars, Mongols, Armenians, Russians, Ukrainians, Jews, etc.

In this unusual mosaic of different social elements comprising Polish society, the Catholic Church played the role of a stabilizing and unifying factor. Let us mention here the Lublin Union of 1569, when one monetary system and one legislative body were established for Lithuania and Poland, solving the problem of the Christianization of Eastern Europe. In 1596 the Brzesc Union returned many millions of members of the Eastern Church into the Catholic faith. Poland also played an important role during the Council of Florence, where the Polish delegation strongly advocated reunion with the Orthodox Church.

---

8   "Chrzescijanin a kultura," *Znak*, 10 (1964), p. 1154.

• THE DIGNITY OF MAN •

Poland has been known as one of the most tolerant countries of Europe. This tolerance is evidenced by several historical events. In 1561 Courland-Livonia, having a choice between Protestant Sweden or Denmark and Catholic Poland, turned to the latter, asking to be included in the Polish commonwealth, where they expected to be granted more liberal self-governance. Significantly, Polish tolerance was extended to include non-Christian religions, as may be shown by the fact that, whenever Jews were persecuted in the West, they took refuge in Poland where they found conditions of tolerance.

While the rest of Europe lived by the principle of *cuius regio, eius religio,* Sigmundus II Augustus (1520-1572) announced in the Polish Diet: "I am your king, but am not king of your conscience."[9] The Crown Chancellor, Jan Zamoyski (1542-1605), wrote to Polish Protestants: "If it could happen that all of you became papists, I would give half of my wealth for it, so that in joining the other half, I could enjoy this holy unity. But, if anyone should do violence to you, I would give all my wealth to you, so that I would not have to look at this bondage."[10] A bill passed by the Polish Diet in 1572 gave equal rights to people of all religious denominations, and provided that no man could be persecuted for his religious beliefs.[11]

This religious tolerance grew from the spirit of freedom. In the name of religious freedom Polish delegates at the Council of Constance called for the suppression of the Teutonic Knights' heresy, according to which one could use force and power in the Christianization of pagans or nonbelievers. At this council the leader of the Polish delegation, Paul Vladimir Wlodkowicz, remonstrated against Falkenberg's doctrine: "It is not permitted to convert pagans to Christianity by sword and

---

[9] Pawel Jasienica, *Polska Jagiellonow* (Warszawa: Panstwowy Instytut Wydawniczy, 1967), p. 177.

[10] Françoise Moal, "Tolerance in Poland: Political Choice and Tradition," in *Tradition of Polish Ideals,* W. J. Stankiewicz, ed. (London, 1981), p. 80.

[11] Anatol Lewicki, *Zarys historii Polski* (London: Orbis, 1947), p. 193.

violence, because this would hurt our neighbor. It is not allowed to seek good ends by doing evil."[12] Wlodkowicz was in agreement with Stanislaus of Skalmierz, who in 1411 wrote a treatise entitled *Concerning Just Wars,* in which he condemned wars of aggression, at the same time affirming the responsibility of a nation to defend itself against any aggressor. He also stressed the necessity of maintaining friendly relations with neighboring states, regardless of their internal policies.

These lofty expressions of Wlodkowicz and Stanislaus of Skalmierz did not remain pure and ideal proclamations, but were put into practice. When the followers of Huss, who was condemned at the Council of Constance for his teachings, were finally defeated in Bohemia and Moravia, they found not only refuge in Poland, but enjoyed there full religious freedom, e.g., the activities of Commenius.

Condemnation of violence is only a negative characteristic of the spirit of freedom. The true nature of freedom is based on the principle of brotherhood and charity. In the proclamation of the Union of Horodlo in 1413, on the basis of which Poland and Lithuania merged into one commonwealth, we read:

> It is universally acknowledged that no one will attain salvation, who is not inspired by the mystery of charity, a virtue which never errs, but radiates its own goodness; it reconciles the men at variance with one another, reunites these opposed, subdues hatred, appeases wrath, and nurtures man upon the bread of peace; charity gathers together the dispersed, comforts the oppressed, soothes the rough, makes the misshapen upright, strengthens all virtues, and without harming anyone, enfolds all with compassion, so that whosoever seeks shelter under her wings finds a haven and will not fear the assault of anyone. Through her laws flourish, by her kingdoms are governed, with her help cities maintain order, and the whole republic is attaining a higher state.

---

[12] *Polska mysl demokratyczna w ciagu wiekow,* Manfred Kridl, Wladyslaw Malinowski and Jozef Wittlin, ed. (New York, 1945), p. 9.

> Charity among all the virtues takes the foremost place, and whosoever scorns her, will forfeit everything.[13]

Inspired by the Polish past, Karol Wojtyla sees the very essence of ecumenism in Christian charity. Christian charity, however, in the eyes of Wojtyla the theologian, is most fully realized in the church itself. Consequently then, ecumenical consciousness should be based on a proper understanding of the nature of the church as the Mystical Body of Christ.

III

In the history of catholic theology, in regard to its ecclesiology, two conflicting tendencies and radically opposed views on the nature of Christ's Church on earth can be distinguished, namely the absolutistic and the relativistic attitudes. Theological absolutism contemplates the reality of God's Kingdom on earth from the perspective of supernatural life exclusively, and considers the Church primarily as a community unchangeable in its nature and consequently everlasting; as a *sua generis* reality, independent from the actual situation of the world. Theological relativism, on the other hand, attempts to consider the reality of God's Kingdom on earth from the perspective of temporary life, defining the Church as a community of faithful living in a specific historical situation. A community is endowed, however, in an intangible manner, with the charisma of the presence of the Holy Spirit.

The basic difference between the absolutistic and the relativistic views on the nature of the Church pertains to the evaluation of the ways to realize God's Message in the consciousness of men, and in the manifestation of the Heavenly Kingdom on earth.

---

[13] *Ibid.*, p. 5.

The absolutistic *com*prehension of the nature of the Church is ontologically oriented and evaluates the problem of realization of the Heavenly Kingdom on earth as a centrifugal movement, that is outwardly from its center. In its essence, 'center', Christ's Church is beyond all dimensions of time and space, and as such is excluded from all the laws which apply to any changes in the temporal order. The innermost structure of Christ's Church is unchangeable and is not subjected to any essential developments or modifications; the developments which take place apply to the human comprehension of Christ's message alone.[14] The Church, as established by God in accordance to Christ's declaration that "my kingdom is not of this world" (John 18:36), does not belong to the earth alone. Christ's Church so understood becomes the Church of the Message of the Good News--the Church of confession and fidelity to the deposit of faith.

The followers of theological relativism *ap*-prehend the nature of the Church as phenomenologically oriented and evaluate the essence of the Church as an 'anonymous' community of faithful,[15] in which the Will of God manifests Itself in every human person, independently from any cultural or denominational form. The anonymous character of Christian religion brought about a change in understanding the Church as an unchangeable, visible institution to one of a community of faithful, possessing however, an invisible character. The Church, as a manifestation of God Himself established by Christ, through His act of eternal salvation, encompasses all men and all social bodies of faithful. Consequently, it is forever changing, both in time and space. The nature of the Church so considered, lies in the 'catholicity' of all religions of the world in the sense of the religious experience of all mankind, inde-

---

[14] Cf. Karl Adam, *The Spirit of Catholicism* (New York: The Macmillan Co., 1933).

[15] On the conception of 'anonymity of Christianity' see: Karl Rahner, *Sendung und Gnade* (Innsbruck: Tyrolia Verlag, 1959).

pendently of any denominational institutions or forms. The basic attributes of Christ's Church consist of the Charisma of the presence of the Holy Spirit. It is this charismatic character of Christ's Church that constitutes the basis for the ecumenical movement, since the deposit of faith and salvation cannot be appropriated by any one community of faithful exclusively, but represents a common gain of all those who believe in God. As such, the Church is a Church of witnessing through an awareness of the solidarity of all men.[16]

The fact of the existing possibility of a twofold interpretation of the nature of Christ's Church in the catholic ecclesiology stems from the teaching of Christology regarding the twofold nature of Christ Himself, both as God and Man.[17] Since Church in fact is Christ Himself, and since Christ is God-Man, therefore the Church as Christ living among men contains in Herself both divine and human elements. From the perspective of the doctrine proclaiming the Church as a divine and human community, there is a possibility of overstressing the teaching about Christ, one or the other aspect, as it already

---

[16] Cf. Gregory Baum, "The Ecclesial Reality of the Other Churches", *Concilium* 4 (1965), pp. 62-86; *Faith and Doctrine* (Paramus, N.J.: Newman Press, 1969), *Man's Becoming* (New York: Herder, 1970); Leslie Dewart, *Theological Foundations* (New York: Herder, 1969); cf. also Richard P. McBrien, *Do We Need the Church* (New York and Evanston: Harper and Row, 1969), pp. 14-15: "The Church is no longer to be conceived as the center of God's plan of salvation. Not all men are called to membership in the Church, nor is such membership a sign of present salvation or a guarantee of future salvation. The central reality is not the Church but the Kingdom of God... All men are called to the Kingdom; not all men are called to the Church."

[17] Yves Marie J. Congar, *Sainte Eglise* (Paris: Ed. du Cerf, 1963), pp. 69-104; Ferdinand Holböck, "Das Mysterium der Kirche in dogmatischer Sicht", in *Mysterium Kirche in der Sicht der theologischen Disziplinen*, I (Salzburg: O. Müller, 1962), publ. by F. Holböck and Thomas Sartory, pp. 234ff. On various interpretations of the Church, see: Avery Dulles, *Models of the Church* (New York: Doubleday, 1974); Thomas Franklin O'Meara, "Philosophical Models in Ecclesiology", *Theological Studies*, 1 (1978), pp. 3-21. On the historical development of viewing the nature of the Church, see: Eric G. Jay, *The Church: Its Changing Image Through Twenty Centuries* (London: SPCK, 1978).

took place in the earliest times of Christianity. We can distinguish here two perils threatening the catholic ecclesiology, namely Docetism and Monophysitism on the one hand, and Nestorianism and Photinianism on the other hand.

Both ecclesiological Docetism and Monophysitism either negate the very human element in the Church as such, or reduce the divine and human character of the Church to the realm of divine dimensions, consequently obliterating any differences which exist between them. Ecclesiological Nestorianism, on the one hand, by overstressing the human reality in the Church, often leads to the isolation of these two realities in the Church. This is exemplified by the distinction between the Roman Catholic Church and the Mystical Body of Christ, proclaimed in earlier times. Pope Leo XIII warned against these perils in his encyclical *"Satis cognitum"*:

> As Christ Himself cannot become known to us in His entirety, when, following Nestorianism and Photinianism, instead of accepting both of His natures, only His human or divine nature separately is considered, so also the Mystical Body of Christ can only become the true Church when both of these realities, that is, divine and human will be accepted.[18]

In the interpretation of the duality of the Church as both a divine and human reality, we note specific ways of understanding the inner structure of the Church among theologians.[19] Previously, theologians who stressed the divine origin of the Church found themselves in need of a 'concretization' of the reality of God's grace. Consequently, in defining the inner structure of the Church they indicated in contrast to the protestant theologians, to Her visible character. One classical example of that attitude in the catholic

---

[18] *Acta Apostolicae Sedis*, 28 (1896), p. 710.
[19] Regarding the evolution of views on the nature of the Church with bibliography, cf. Romuald Gustaw OFM, "Pojecie i charakter historii Kosciola", in *Pod Tchnieniem Ducha Swietego* (Poznan-Warszawa-Lublin: Sw. Wojciech, 1964), pp. 383ff.

ecclesiology is the well-known definition formulated by Bellarmine:

> The one and true Church, is a group of men bound together by the profession of the same sacraments, under the rule of the legitimate pastors, and especially of the one vicar of Christ on earth, the Roman pontiff. From this definition it can easily be gathered which men belong to the Church, and which do not... For the Church is a group of men as visible and palpable as that of the Roman people, or the Kingdom of France, or the Republic of Venice.[20]

Contemporary theologians, starting from the more 'human' character of the Church, attempt to penetrate the divine structure of the reality of Christ's grace and discover God's plan for every man: one example of such an attitude in today's ecclesiology is the definition of the Church proposed by M. Schmaus: "The Church is the by Christ established New Testament People of God, hierarchically constituted, dedicated to the reign of God and the salvation of man, existing as the full of mystery Body of Christ."[21]

The twofold character of the Church as both human and divine realities consists of a specific tension between the order of grace and nature. However, this tension between the order of grace and nature should not be understood in the sense of an ontological contradiction between the two different realities

---

[20] "De consiliis et ecclesia", 1, III, c. 2; *Opera Omnia* (Parisiis, 1872), II, p. 75: "Coetum hominum eiusdem christianae fidei professione et eorundum sacramentorum communione colligatum, sub regimine legitimorum pastorum ac praecipue unius Christi vicarii Romani Pontificis... ecclesia enim est coetus hominum ita visibilis et palpabilis ut est coetus populi romani vel regnum Galliae aut respublica Venetorum." This radically legalistic understanding of the nature of the Church is, however, not exclusively Bellarmine's, cf. F. Malmberg, *Een Lichaam en een Geest* (Utrecht: Spectrum, 1958), pp. 24-25.

[21] *Katolische Dogmatik*, III (München: Max Hueber Verlag, 1958), p. 48; cf. also Karl Rahner, *Theology of Pastoral Action* (New York: Herder, 1968), pp. 26-27: "The Church is the community, legitimately constituted in a social structure, in which through faith, hope and love God's eschatologically definitive revelation (his self-communication) in Christ remains present for the world as a reality and truth."

since the ultimate author of both of these orders is God Himself. The tension which exists in the Church between human nature and divine grace consists in the dialectics between Christ's act of Redemption and the means of realizing the act of eternal salvation among men. The act of Redemption is the unchanging and stable element in the Church, since it has been fulfilled by Christ Himself through His Crucifixion and Resurrection. The act of eternal salvation, however, is the changeable element in the Church, since it depends on the free acceptance of grace by every individual and particular man.

The dialectics of tension between nature and grace in the Church consist then of a specific polarization of the two orders: natural and supernatural. In the supernatural order the Church remains a reality which is unchangeable and eternal. In the natural order, the Church is changeable, depending on the conditions of a given time and space. The perils facing oldtime theologians led to a breach of unity between the natural and supernatural order,[22] and to the uprooting of the Church from human reality. The dangers of contemporary theology lie in the opposite direction, that is, in obliterating the distinction between the Church and human reality.[23] In order to establish a proper balance between the divine and the human elements in the Church, the specific structure of the Church has to be brought into focus.

The basic causes for the dialectical tension between nature and grace can be found in the relationship between men and

---

[22] The previous understanding of the Church as the Mystical Body of Christ led to overly juxtaposing of the "body" to "people"; cf. M. D. Koster, *Ekklesiologie im Werden* (Paderborn: Bonifacius Drm. 1940); L. Cerfaux, *La Théologie de l'Eglise suivant Saint Paul* (Paris: Ed. du Cerf), 1942. For an evaluation of the literature dealing with the Church as God's People, cf. Rudolph Schnackenburg and Jacques Dupont, "The Church as the People of God", *Concilium* 1 (1964), pp. 117-129.

[23] The errors in contemporary catholic ecclesiology found in some theologians of today consist mainly in a tendency toward a reduction of the nature of the Church to the meaning of God's People. Cf. Gregory Baum, *Man's Becoming*, ch. 2, "Redemptive immanence."

God.[24] From the point of view of the attitude of men towards God, the Church presents Herself as the People of God, endowed by the Holy Ghost with a spirit of all-human solidarity in Christ the Savior.[25] The Church, as God's creation, emerges as the Mystical Body of Christ, uniting all faithful into one organism of a supernatural community.[26] These two aspects of the nature of the Church demand an equilibrium between God's People and Christ's Body to be established and preserved.[27] In relation to this, R. Schnackenburg writes:

> The Church in the New Testament remains God's people but it is a people of God newly constituted in Christ and in relation to Christ... The Church is the people of God as the Body of Christ, in a sense which is determined by, or at least grounded on, the idea of the people of God.[28]

---

[24] About the mutual relationship between the Church and the human race, cf. S. H. Schillebeeckxs "The Church and Makind", *Concilium* 1 (1964), pp. 69-101.

[25] Cf. Yves Marie J. Congar, "The People of God", in *Vatican II* (Notre Dame: University of Notre Dame Press, 1966), pp. 197-202.

[26] Cf. Yves Marie J. Congar, *Esquisses du mystere de l'Eglise* (Paris: Ed. du Cerf, 1953). Cf. also Yves de Montcheuil, *Aspects de l'Eglise* (Paris: Ed. du Cerf, 1956), pp. 32ff.

[27] J. Backes, "Die Kirche is das Volk Gottes im Neuen Bund", *Trierer Theologische Zeitschrift* 69 (1960), pp. 111- 117; "Gottesvolk im Neuen Bund", *Trierer Theologische Zeitschrift* 70 (1961), pp. 80-93; L. Bouyer, "Ou en est la théologie du Corps Mystique?", *Revue des Sciences Religieuse* 22 (1948), pp. 313ff; cf. also Henryk Bogacki, "Misterium Kosciola Pielgrzymujacego", in *Kosciol w swietle Soboru*, ed. by H. Bogacki, and S. Moysa (Poznan: Sw. Wojciech, 1968), p. 64: "W ten sposob wylania sie koniecznosc dopelnienia okreslenia Kosciola jako 'Ludu Bozego' przez pojecie 'Ciala Chrystusowego'."

[28] *Die Kirche im Neuen Testament* (Freiburg: Herder, 1961), p. 147. Cf. also Nils Alstrup Dahl, *Das Volk Gottes: eine Untersuchung zum Kirchenbewusstein des Unchristentums*, 2 Aufl. (Darmstadt: Wissenschaftliche Buchgesellschaft, 1963), pp. 225-226: "Sächlich ist der Kirchenbegriff des Paulus aber derselbe ob er nun vom 'Volke Gottes' oder vom 'Leibe Christi' spricht. Der 'Leib Christi' wird durch die Sakramente konstituerit und dadurch durch das Christusgeschehen... Wir dürfen also darauf schliessen dass der Begriff 'Leib Christi' eine besondere Ausprägung der Vorstellung vom neuen Volke Gottes und nicht ein damit konkurierender Gedanke ist."

The complex structure of the Church as a reality, both divine and human, requires from theologians a differentiation of the various elements, both stable and changeable, temporal and eternal, visible and spiritual.[29] The Church, as a divine reality established by Christ Himself, is in Her very structure unchangeable and eternal.[30] As a human reality, the Church is changeable in Her structure and is subjected to different modifications, depending on time and space.[31] Pope Paul VI pointed to this image of the Church as presented in the teaching of Vatican II relating to the Pilgrim Church: "The image of the pilgrim age points to the twofold life of the Church: one in time, that is in time in which we are finding ourselves at present, the other beyond time, in eternity, meaning that to which our pilgrimage is leading us."[32]

The essence of the Pilgrim Church consists in the striving of fallen mankind towards the 'fulness of grace in Christ':

> The pilgrim Church in her sacraments and institutions, which pertain to this present time, takes on the appearance of the passing world. She herself dwells among creatures who groan and

---

[29] Cf. Bertrand van Bilsen, *The Changing Church* (Pittsburg: Duquesne University Press, 1966), pp. 11-13; Charles Journet, *L'Eglise du Verbe Incarne: II, sa structure interne et son unité catholique* (Paris: Descle du Brouwer, 1951), pp. 8 ff, 40, 44-49; Henri de Lubac, *Méditation sur L'Eglise*, 3 éd. (Paris: Aubier, 1954), pp. 77ff; Theo Westow, *The Agony of the Church* (London-Sidney: Sheed and Ward, 1968), pp. 22-38.

[30] St. Thomas, *S.th.*, III, 8, 5 ad 1.

[31] The complexity of the Church is also evidenced by the twofold meaning in the etymology of the Greek word *ekklesia*; in the Greek language we have two expressions: *kiriakon* (the community of Lord) and *kiriake ekklesia* (the community of the Lord); cf. Louis Bouyer, *Dictionary of Theology* (Descle Co., Inc., 1965), p. 81. Previous theology used mainly the first expression in regard to the Church and consequently stressed the visible character of the Church; cf. William E. Addis and Thomas Arnold, *A Catholic Dictionary* (St. Louis: B. Herder Book Co., 1960), pp. 175ff. The contemporary theologians conceive the Church as People of God, and thus stress the invisible character of the Church; cf. Yves Marie J. Congar, *Esquisses*.

[32] *La Documentation Catholique* 67 no. 1564 (1970), p. 513. Regarding the development of Church theology before Vatican II, cf. George H. Tavard, *The Pilgrim Church* (New York: Herder, 1967), ch. I, pp. 15-41.

travail in pain until now and await the revelation of the sons of God.33

Man's pilgrimage understood in those terms points to the eschatological character of the calling within the Church:

> "The Church, to which we are called in Christ Jesus, and in which we acquire sanctity through the grace of God, will attain her full perfection only in the glory of heaven. Then will come the time of the restoration of all things. Then the human race as well as the entire world, which is intimately related to man and acquires its purpose through him, will be perfectly re-established in Christ."34

The ultimate destiny of all men in the attainment of eternal life assigns to the Church Her character of the 'universal sacrament of salvation':35

> The Church then, God's only flock, like a standard lifted high for the nations to see, ministers the gospel of peace to all mankind...as she makes her pilgrim way in hope towards her goal, her fatherland above.36

The Pilgrim Church as a universal sacrament of salvation also becomes: "...the Church is a kind of sacrament or sign of intimate union with God, and of the unity of all mankind,"37 and consequently acquires the characteristics of Christian ecumenism.

Following the teaching of Vatican II, catholic theology presents the Church in Her pilgrimage as a community endowed with an eschatological,38 sacramental,39 and ecumenical

---

33 "Dogmatic Constitution on the Church", in *The Documents of Vatican II*, p. 79.
34 *Ibid.*, p. 78.
35 *Ibid.*
36 "Decree on Ecumenism", *The Documents of Vatican II*, p. 344.
37 "Dogmatic Constitution on the Church", *The Documents of Vatican II*, p. 15.
38 Barnabas Ahern, "The Eschatological Dimensions of the Church", *Vatican II*, pp. 293-300; P. Molinari, "Der Endzeitliche Character der pilgernden Kirche und ihre Einheit mit der himmlischen Kirche", in: *De Ecclesia, Beiträge zur Konstitution 'über der Kirche' des Zweiten Vatikanischen Konzils II* (Freiburg: Herder, 1966), pp. 449- 456; Wolfhart Pannenberg, "The Significance of Eschatology for the Understanding of the

character.⁴⁰ The eschatological character of the Church denotes the complexity of the temporal reality, subjugated to the demands of future, eternal life.⁴¹ The sacramental character refers to the unification of the visible and the invisible elements in the Church.⁴² And finally, the ecumenical character stresses the unity in plurality.⁴³ These three components of the Church are integrally connected with each other and signify the complex character of divine reality on earth.

Apostolicity and Catholicity of the Church", *One in Christ* 6 (1970), pp. 410-429; R. Ruether, *The Church Against Itself: An Inquiry into the Conditions of Historical Existence for the Eschatological Community* (New York: Herder, 1967), pp. 50-65; Thomas A. Sartory, *The Oecumenical Movement and the Unity of the Church* (Westminster, Md.; Newman Press, 1963), pp. 128-140; Ruldolph Schnackenburg, "Church and Parousia", in *One, Holy, Catholic, and Apostolic: Studies in the Nature and Role of the Church in the Modern World*, public. by Herbert Vorgrimler (London: Sheed and Ward, 1968), pp. 91-134; *idem*, "Wesenzüge und Geheimnis der Kirche nach Neuen Testament", in *Mysterium Kirche*, p. 138ff.

39 Odo Brooke, "The Church: Sacrament of Mankind in Christ", *The American Benedictine Review* 21 (1970), pp. 79- 87; Jan Groot, "The Church as Sacrament of the World", *Concilium* 31 (1967), pp. 51-66; Gerard Philips, "The Church: Mystery and Sacrament", *Vatican II*, pp. 187-196; John Powell, *The Mystery of the Church* (Milwaukee: The Bruce Pub. Co., 1967), pp. 62-70; Karl Rahner, *Kirche und Sakramente* (Freiburg: Herder, 1963); Edward Schillebeeckxs, *Le Christ, Sacrament de la recontre de Dieu* (Paris: Ed. du Cerf, 1960); O. Semmelroth, *Die Kirche als Ursakrament* (Frankfurt: Joseph Knecht, 1963); Jan Witte, "Some Thesis about the Sacramentality of the Church", *One in Christ* 6 (1970), pp. 390-409.

40 Hans Küng, *Strukturen der Kirche* (Freiburg: Herder, 1962).

41 Cf. Jürgen Moltmann, *Theology of Hope* (London: SCM Press Ltd., 1967), p. 16: "From the first to last, and not merely in the epilogue, Christianity is eschatology, is hope, forward looking and forward moving, and therefore also revolutionizing and transforming the presence. The eschatological... is the medium of Christian faith as such.... There is therefore only one real problem in christian theology...: the problem of the future."

42 Hans Urs von Balthasar, *Church and World* (New York: Herder, 1967); S. C. Butter, *The Theology of Vatican II* (London-Darton: Longman and Todd, 1967).

43 Card. Paul-Emile Léger, "Freedom and Diversity", in *Council Speeches of Vatican II*, ed. by Hans Küng, Yves Congar, Daniel O'Hanlon (Glen Rock, N.J.: Paulist Press, 1964), pp. 222-225; Card. Alfrink, "Unity and Plurality

The vision of the Church as a community in pilgrimage towards eternity opens new perspectives for contemporary theological inquiry such as: the issue of the unity of all Christians in the Church; the problem of the universal membership of all human race in the Church;[44] the question of the values of temporal life,[45] and so on.

IV

Referring to the teaching of Vatican II, Wojtyla remarks that the church in its teaching not only advocates ecumenism but, through its doctrine of the church as the universal people of God, it, in fact, expresses ecumenism in its broadest sense.[46] Christ's church understood as the universal people of God becomes, by the same token, "the principle of all ecumenism"[47] and consists of a unity of all people in Christ. Wojtyla refers to St. Paul, comparing the church to the human body which, although comprised of many different members and organs, is still enlivened by one spirit, thus creating a unity.[48]

The universalistic understanding of the ecumenical consciousness leads Wojtyla to distinguish in the church between

---

in the Church", *The American Ecclesiastical Review* 161 (1969), pp. 128-135.

[44] Previous theology referred to the membership in the Church under the conditions of: baptism, the confession of faith and ecclesiastical authority; cf. Pius XII "Mystici Corporis", *Acta Apostolicae Sedis*, 35 (1943), pp. 193-248. In the present time one refers to the membership to the Church under the conditions of grace, faith, sacraments, authority of the Church and community; cf. "Lumen gentium", *Acta Apostolicae Sedis* 57 (1965), ch. 1-2. Cf. also Colman O'Neil, "Membership in the Church", *The American Ecclesiastical Review* 160 (1969), pp. 363-375.

[45] Hans Urs von Balthasar, *Church and World*.

[46] *Sources of Renewal* (San Francisco: Harper & Row, 1980), p. 310.

[47] *Kazania*, p. 372.

[48] *Ibid.*, p. 388.

the objective and subjective aspect of the unity of all people in Christ. This twofold aspect of unity is a consequence of the very nature of the church as being both temporal and eternal, human and divine. Moreover, since the church is in fact Christ himself and since Christ is the God-Man, the church as Christ living among men therefore contains in itself both a divine and a human element. In view of this Wojtyla concludes:

> This consciousness on the Church's part results, we may say, from the manner in which God has revealed Himself, as a unity and yet a community of persons. In accepting this revelation men are not only confronted with a reality which is God in Himself, but at the same time find that they have been led into the depths of this mysterious, supernatural reality and thus that their vocation is to be united with God.[49]

The twofold character of the Church as both human and divine realities reflects a tension between the orders of grace and nature. This tension, however, should not be understood as an ontological contradiction between the two different realities, since the ultimate author of both of these orders is God himself. The tension existing in the church between human nature and divine grace is actually a dialectic between Christ's act of redemption and the means of realizing the act of eternal salvation among men. The act of redemption is the unchanging and stable element in the church, since it has been fulfilled by Christ himself through his crucifixion and resurrection. The act of eternal salvation, however, is the changeable element in the church since it depends on the free acceptance of grace by every individual and particular person.

Speaking of redemption and salvation, Wojtyla refers to the fact that Christ died on the cross so that all people could be saved. The act of salvation, then, is the unifying element not only of the church but of all humanity. The dynamics of salvation, that is, the dynamics of grace which stem from Christ himself, touches the human soul in different ways,

---

[49] *Sources of Renewal*, p. 55.

forming thus the Mystical Body of Christ.[50]

The dialectic tension between nature and grace in the church is a specific polarization of the two orders, natural and supernatural. In the supernatural order, the church remains a reality which is unchangeable and eternal. In the natural order, the church is changeable, depending on concrete circumstances. Commenting on the nature of the church as the universal sacrament of salvation, Wojtyla writes:

> In Jesus Christ both dimensions of the Church, the temporal and the eschatological, are not only in unity but interpenetrate each other. The eschatological community of the Church is formed continually in a lively union with the aims of the pilgrim Church on earth. The centre and source of that union is Christ.[51]

Unity in Christ is then both the objective and the subjective element of ecumenical consciousness. In the spirit of this twofold element, ecumenical consciousness would consist in striving for the unity of all men--unity not only within the church or, for that matter, unity within Christianity as such, but a unity of all mankind. This is unity which rejects any

---

[50] *Kazania*, p. 352: "This source is to be found in the mystery of salvation. We strongly believe that Christ, the Son of God, the Eternal Word, became Man and died on the Cross in order to save all people. Unity is, therefore, contained in the act of salvation, so to speak, beforehand as a principle or foundation. The act of salvation in its deepest sense embraces all men. It is intended for them and tries to reach all of them. And if we are based on the mystery of salvation, then we see not only the unity of the church but the unity of all humanity in this one act, in this mystery and in the person who is Christ, the redeemer of all men, who in the mystery of salvation embraces all men. The mystery of salvation has its own dynamics, the dynamics stemming from Christ himself--the God-Man. This dynamics is the dynamics of grace. Grace reaches human souls in different ways because there is salvation. Thus, on the foundation of salvation there is formed that which we call the Mystical Body of Christ--the penetration of the human soul, the penetration of humanity by sanctifying grace, because the mystery of salvation enters human souls, enters all humanity through grace."

[51] *Sources of Renewal*, p. 183.

conflicts or hatred and hostility, but is instead based on peace, understanding and love.[52]

The common denominator of ecumenical consciousness should be based--according to Wojtyla--on human identity and solidarity, and should be sought in man as a person:

> Thus the ecumenical attitude must be marked in the first place by full respect for human beings, by readiness to meet and cooperate with them, and by a "dialogue" or exchange of opinions on doctrinal matters, which of course presupposes adequate theological preparation. This exchange of opinions, the object of which is to enable the parties to know one another, must above all be prayerful.[53]

V

The ecumenical dialogue cannot, however, be understood as a simple acceptance of the doctrinal differences which exist among separated brothers in Christ. Wojtyla warns us against a false irenicism which would give the impression that Christians are not divided at all.[54] Such an attitude would lead in practice to indifferentism.[55] To avoid dogmatic indifferentism, any ecumenical dialogue must be based on truth.

---

[52] `Aby Chrystus sie nami poslugiwal' (Kraków: Znak, 1979), p. 198: "Christian unity is not just an internal matter for us, not just an internal matter for the Church, not even just an internal matter for all Christianity, for all denominations and all churches. My dear friends, it is a great question for all mankind. If we Christians can manage to meet in peace, if we can manage to become really united, then this will be an enormous lesson of great optimism for all mankind on what man can do, a lesson that human life, the life of humanity, must not be based on conflict and hatred and hostilities, that human life can base itself on peace, on unity, on understanding, on love, and can find a common denominator."

[53] *Sources of Renewal*, p. 318.

[54] *Ibid.*, p. 323.

[55] *Ibid.*, p. 325.

Distinguishing between the vertical and the horizontal orientations, our author observes:

> ...Vatican II assigns primary importance to the former and derives from it the function of the "ecumenical dialogue." The union of Christians can only be the sign of grace, a sign of God's forgiveness which we must first implore and deserve. Only from God can all our efforts on the "horizontal" plane receive the necessary strength and authentic "ecumenical" meaning.[56]

Placing truth as the guiding principle of ecumenical dialogue, Wojtyla does not intend to exclude freedom from the ecumenical movement. On the contrary, he sees freedom as the very condition of each individual discovery of religious truth. It is only through exercising his freedom that man, as a rational being, finds the coherence between truth and reality, and engages himself personally in a relationship with God, accepting as truth the word of God. This acceptance is an expression of faith, and therefore it has a supernatural character. Summarizing his reflections, Wojtyla says: "Man brings his own freedom into religion and commits himself, accepting as truth the word of God and the self-revelation of God which it contains."[57]

In stressing the doctrinal foundation of the ecumenical movement, Wojtyla goes so far as to reach for its roots in the Fatherhood of God and in the universality of man's salvation by Christ's redeeming act. A true ecumenical attitude, however, respects the inner freedom of man and his personal conviction regarding truth. Moreover, this depth of faith in Christ as the redeemer of all men is--in the words of Karol Wojtyla--"the expression of a profound love for man and respect for his inner liberty." This inner liberty is a responsible one and "corresponds to an inward conviction concerning truth."[58]

---

[56] *Ibid.*, p. 321.
[57] *Ibid.*, p. 25.
[58] *Ibid.*, p. 313.

The ecumenical dialogue is, then, based on truth and freedom, but the latter must be subordinated to the former. Freedom, however, should be guided by truth. Thus, ecumenism cannot be satisfied by acceptance of the *status quo*, but must be enhanced and developed by a search for truth.[59] The reason for the supremacy of truth over freedom is the very nature of man:

> Man by his nature possesses freedom, he is endowed with free will. But his freedom is subordinate in man to reason, and through reason to the truth. This freedom does not mean license and arbitrariness, that man is free to profess anything at all, free to believe anything at all, free in religious matters to assert anything at all... And when we Christians, separated brethren, on the one hand declare our mutual respect for each other's convictions, and proclaim religious freedom, we must, on the other hand, at the same time stress the higher laws of truth.[60]

In searching for religious truth in the spirit of freedom, all Christians involved in ecumenical dialogue must show a readiness for conversion. Wojtyla understands conversion from the theological point of view as a divine grace, through which the separated followers of Christ should accept one another. Conversion, therefore, is not only a result of man's intellect and will, but it has a divine dimension. In this respect John Paul II writes:

> Conversion is above all acceptance. It is the effort to accept God in all the riches of His "conversion" to man. This conversion is a Grace. The effort of the intellect, of the heart and of the will is also indispensable for the acceptance of the Grace. It is indispensable not to lose the divine dimension of life in the human dimension; to persevere in it.[61]

Applying the principle of conversion to ecumenical dialogue, Wojtyla defines it as something more than a mere conversation, but as an attitude of openness toward others.

---

[59] "Pope John Paul II at Vatican II," *National Catholic Reporter*, 27 October 1978.
[60] *Kazania*, p. 363.
[61] *Through the Year*, p. 49.

Wojtyla sees in dialogue an ability to express one's thoughts and to listen and understand the other person. This ability should have, of necessity, the characteristic of the reasoning required of man as a social being. Only such an attitude will be deeply Christian, since it will pave the way for mutual understanding and respect and, consequently, for Christian unity.[62]

Ecumenical dialogue based on a readiness for mutual conversion will result in a reconciliation of all Christians into the one organic unity of the church. The bishop of Kraków acknowledges that the future of ecumenism lies both in the hands of God and in the attitudes of man. The unity of Christians cannot be based on and grow from simple mutual tolerance which, in fact, will amount to compromise. Wojtyla reasons: "The Church is not simply a society of people who exercise mutual toleration. The church is an organic unity. It is a body, the Mystical Body of Christ. But the unity of this mystical body, which is also the social unity of all God's people, must gradually grow and ripen, until it is ripe and full."[63]

In summary, Wojtyla concludes that ecumenical dialogue is possible if there are faith, hope and prayer: "The primacy of faith, hope, and prayer is linked with the necessity of spiritual renewal and profound conversion."[64] Our faith will "put an end to the intolerable scandal of Christian division,"[65] our hope is in "seeking paths leading to unity,"[66] our prayers are "a privileged instrument for participation in the pursuit of Christian unity."[67]

---

[62] *Ibid.*, pp. 149-150.
[63] *Ibid.*, p. 151.
[64] *Sources of Renewal*, p. 320.
[65] *Through the Year*, p. 27.
[66] *Ibid.*, p. 143.
[67] *Ibid.*, p. 23.

VI. THE DIGNITY OF BEING HUMAN

When Jacob Burckhart published his book in 1810 entitled *Die Kultur der Renaissance*, Christianity had been accused, because of its anti-humanistic tendencies, of depriving human nature of its unique value and dignity. The main reason for this accusation is the theocentrism of Christian doctrine: if God is the ultimate purpose of all created beings, human beings included, then man is deprived of any specific value and dignity of his own nature. In Christianity, then, there is no room for a true humanism, and equating Christianity with humanism is simply a contradiction in terms. At the heart of the dispute concerning the character of humanism lies the question of human nature and man's ultimate destiny.

The very essence of humanism consists in finding man's dignity. The dignity of man, however, may be sought either in an immanent or in a transcendent order of human nature: in the former, we will have a naturalistic form of humanism, and in the latter, a spiritualistic one. The question arises: how can we resolve this ambiguity of humanism? Karol Wojtyla proposes to analyze the *humanum* and *divinum* in man both by following the historical development of humanistic trends, and by establishing the formal constituent of human nature.

I

In an historical investigation one might distinguish several approaches in understanding human dignity. Basically speaking the whole question of the dignity of man depends on the way one views human nature. If man is only a part of the material world, and if his being does not essentially differ from any other natural things, then human dignity lies entirely in "his relation to nature," as this has been expressed by Karl Marx.[1] But, if there is in man something which surpasses pure matter, then his dignity consists in God, according to the principle formulated by Soren Kierkegaard: The more a man needs God, the more perfect he is.[2]

The question of humanism, then, depends on how we view the destiny of man's life, and whether or not there exists in the human being a need for a set of values that are higher than natural ones. Humanism so conceived has received, in the past, two forms:

a) the pre-Christian view which perceives the dignity of man in his superiority over the animal;

b) the Christian view, which seeks human dignity in the possibility of man's participation in the divine life through grace.

---

[1] *Economic and Philosophic Manuscripts of 1844*, ed. with an introduction by Dirk J. Struik (New York: International Publishers, 1964), p. 134.

[2] *Economic and Philosophic Manuscripts of 1844*, ed. with an introduction by Dirk J. Struik (New York: International Publishers, 1964), p. 134.

The doctrine according to which man is composed of body and soul, and the belief in the superiority of spirit over matter, has its origin in the Orphic tradition. The body, as the element of Titans, is a prison or a tomb of the soul, while the soul, as the divine element which came from Dionysius, came into existence through the breath of the whole. Being composed of body and soul, man is in a state of punishment for some original "sin" committed by the human race. Therefore, the body is sinful and evil, and the soul must be purified by religious rituals and ceremonies.

The first philosopher to introduce the Orphic view of man to philosophy and to evaluate it critically was Socrates. Following the Orphics, Socrates believed that the body element is composed of material stuff, but that the human soul is divine in origin; and because it is divine in origin, the soul can make man good and happy. Therefore man's dignity should be sought in the human soul. Realizing, however, the instability of human nature, Socrates defined the soul as that in virtue of which someone is wise or foolish, good or evil. Socratic humanism, then, consists in searching for human dignity through the improvement of the goodness of the human soul.

These original insights which sought human dignity in the spiritual realm, were fully developed in antiquity by Plato and Aristotle. In his dialogue *Alcibiades* I Plato writes: "Man is one of three things: soul, body, or the union of the two."[3] The highest unity of man lies in his spirit, for "the spiritual (love) is intermediate between the divine and the mortal."[4] Because of its spiritual dimension, the human soul has its beginning in divinity: "Man, having a share in the spiritual attributes, is the only of the animals, who has any gods, because he alone is of their kindred; and he raises altars and images of them."[5]

---

3   130a.
4   *Symposium*, 202e.
5   *Protagoras*, 322a.

Consequently, the dignity of man consists, according to Plato, in having a soul which "is the most divine"[6] element in the whole of reality.

Although Aristotle placed men among animals--in agreement with his doctrine on the hylomorphic structure of things--he nevertheless sees in man some dimensions which surpass the realm of pure materiality, when he defines "man as the only animal that is erect, because his nature and essence are divine."[7] Moreover, man's soul is "in a way all existing things,"[8] because through "the cognitive powers of his active intellect, man can elevate to immateriality and eternity his own self..."[9] Arriving at this conclusion the Stagirite elaborated on his famous definition of man as a rational animal. However, man's dignity does not lie entirely in his intellect, but in his virtuous conduct, "we call man good, when he is of perfect nature."[10] In commenting on Aristotle's humanism, Maritain writes: "/For Aristotle/to propose to man only the human...is to betray man, and to wish him misfortune, because by the principal part of him, which is the spirit, man is called to be better than purely, human life."[11]

Although, generally speaking, the ancient thinkers proclaimed the superiority of man over animals, and searched for the dignity of man in spirit which transcends pure nature, their humanism, nevertheless, was tragic in nature and heroic in character (Homer, Sophocles, Aeschylus, Euripedes, Virgil, Epictetus, Marcus Aurelius, etc.). The tragic heroism of the ancient thinkers originated in their fatalistic views of nature

---

[6] *Laws*, V: 726.
[7] *De Partibus Animalium*, IV, 10:686a27-28.
[8] *De Anima*, III, 8: 431b20.
[9] *Ibid.*, III, 5: 430a24-25.
[10] *Politica*, III, 4: 1276b33-34.
[11] *Integral Humanism* (New York: Charles Scribner's Sons, 1968), p. 2.

and of man as being only under the law.[12] In other words, the humanism of antiquity depended on the way the thinkers resolved the dialectical tension between *physis* and *nomos*. On the one hand, we have Protagoras' principle of man being the measurement of all things, and on the other, Plato's divine law. (The Stoics also identified fate with *logos* and divine providence--*pronoia*.)

Fatalistic humanism was superseded by the Christian doctrine of redemption. Redeemed nature in man, however, was challenged by "the heritage of original sin"--to use Maritain's expression.[13] Although Christ's grace redeemed human nature from original sin, nevertheless man remained "wounded in his nature."[14] Consequently, man has been viewed as being in a constant tension between natural and supernatural forces, namely, between freedom and grace. But the issue of freedom brought the question of predestination with two possible solutions, namely that of the followers of Banez and that of Molina.

The Protestant movement reinforced the Augustinian tradition of the doctrine of freedom and grace. The radical reformers (Luther, Calvin, and Jansenius) evaluated man as being essentially corrupt by original sin, which, in consequence, deprived him of his freedom. Therefore, Protestant humanism proclaimed "grace without freedom."[15] Maritain underscores the radical consequences of the most extreme position of Calvinism when he writes:

> Calvinism is the best known illustration of (sc. grace without freedom). And we are still in presence of the same antinomy: man is bound down, annihilated under despotic decrees. But the predestined one is sure of his salvation. Thus he is ready to

---

[12] In Greek: *heimarmene*--'fate,' and *nomos*--'law:' only in later Greek philosophy *heimarmene* has been separated from *theos*.
[13] *Ibid.*, p. 10.
[14] *Ibid.*
[15] *Ibid.*, p. 17.

confront anything here below and to conduct himself as the elect of God on earth; his imperialist demands (he who is substantially soiled, but saved still sullied by the sin of Adam, but the elect of God) will be limitless; and material prosperity will seem to him a duty of his state.[16]

The dichotomy between freedom and grace led gradually to the undermining of confidence in Christian humanism, and the attention of thinkers shifted from *divinum* to *humanum*. This attitude can be found in such philosophies as the naturalism of Rousseau, the positivism of Comte, or the idealism of Hegel. According to these philosophers, man is not affected by original sin and he is basically good in his nature. As a result, this optimistic view of human nature paved the road to contemporary anthropomorphic humanism.

Anthropomorphic humanism attempts to evaluate human dignity by eliminating any divine element in man's spirituality, and to treat man as a purely natural being. This naturalistic approach to man has been best expressed by Walter Lippmann who expects from men that they "must find the tests of righteousness wholly within human experience...(and) they must live ...in the belief, that the duty of man is not to make his will conform to the will of God, but to the surest knowledge of the condition of human happiness."[17] A very similar attitude can be found in F.C.S. Schiller, who gives the following definition of humanism: "Humanism is merely the perception that the philosophic problem concerns human beings striving to comprehend a world of human experience by the resources of the human mind."[18]

---

[16] *Ibid.*
[17] *A Preface to Morals* (New York: Macmillan Company, 1929), p. 137.
[18] "Pragmatism and Humanism", in: *Studies in Humanism* (London: Macmillan Company, 1912), p. 12.

II

A historical review of various kinds of humanisms shows that in searching for human dignity, there are two main attitudes: namely, theocentric and anthropocentric. In trying to find a balance between *humanum* and *divinum*, Karol Wojtyla attempts to re-evaluate Christian humanism by finding a new dimension to the eternal question of the dignity of being human. However, by taking into consideration the attitude of contemporary man, Wojtyla tries to base Christian humanism on human experience, thereby finding in it the *divinum*, and formulating a new kind of personalism. The personalism which will lay a new foundation for Christian humanism tries to answer not so much the question "what" man is, as "who" man is.

In asking the question "who is man" (Ps 8:5) the Psalmist expressed the perennial concern of every human being. But the answers to this question are most controversial, and any given answer will inevitably lead to new inquiries into the meaning of human life. From the time of Socrates to contemporary thinkers, philosophers are discovering new dimensions of human reality. The reason for this lies in the fact that "man is so broad, motley, and various a thing, that the definitions of him, all fall a little short."[19] In agreement with the above description given by Max Scheler, Heidegger observes: "(The) perplexity of man increases to immeasurable dimensions."[20]

But, if man cannot be adequately defined in his nature, then instead of evaluating his human reality in his essential characteristics as individual substance, we may try to describe man in his existential dimensions as a subsistent subject of

---

[19] *Zűr Idee des Menschen, Abhandlungen und Aufsätzen*, v. 1 (1915), p. 319; in the second and third editions, the volumes have been published under the title *Vom Umsturz der Werte*.

[20] *Platons Lehre von der Warhheit. Mit einen Brief über den "Humanismus"* (Bern: A. Francke, 1947), p. 104.

actions. In his article, "Thomistic Personalism," Karol Wojtyla writes: "Man is an individual being (*individua substantia*) endowed with individual nature. However, this rational nature does not possess its own subsistence as a nature, but it subsists in a person. Person, then, is the subsisting subject of existence and actions, which cannot be attributed to rational nature."[21] Thus, following Wojtyla we must view man not only as a part of nature (*homo natura*) but also and specifically as a unique person (*homo persona*).

The concept of *persona* belongs uniquely to Western civilization. It was formulated during the Trinitarian and Christological disputes in the early Church. Referring to this historical fact Wojtyla writes: "The <u>category of the person</u> was formulated in the first centuries of Christianity...in order to facilitate to some degree the understanding of the divine: '*divinum.*' Today, after many centuries the category of a person constitutes a key question in the contemporary controversy on the human: '*humanum.*'"[22] In his attempt to resolve the controversy between *humanum* and *divinum* in human life, Wojtyla bases his anthropology on the principle of transcendental teleology. If the purpose of human life is contained in nature alone, then man does not have any other purpose beyond himself, and he is doomed to become a "*passion inutile*" as expressed by Sartre.[23] But, if man's life and actions can be aimed beyond his own nature, then man can transcend the limits of his beingness and his *humanum* can be penetrated by the *divinum*. In one of his early articles, "Humanism and the Purpose of Man," Wojtyla states: "The heart of the matter is in this case the problematics of the purpose. Is God the goal of man, and, if so, in what sense?... Creatures are the act of God's will. Will is always directed toward a goal and the goal of the

---

21 "Personalism tomistyczny," *Znak*, 5 (1961), p. 666.
22 "Il problema del costituirsi della cultura attraverso la 'praxis' umana," *Rivista di filosofia neo-scolastica*, 49 (1977), p. 515.
23 *L'être et le néant* (Paris: Gallimard, 1943), p. 708.

will is always some good. Since the good contained in an objective (that is, a created being) cannot perfect God, it can, therefore, only reveal God."[24]

The principle of transcendental teleology, however, depends on an adequate understanding of man as a person. In his first book, *Evaluation of Possibilities of Building Christian Ethics on the Principles of Max Scheler*,[25] Wojtyla turns to Scheler's anthropology, hoping to find in his personalism the transcendental dimensions of human values. Now it is well known that Scheler's philosophy is person-oriented and it regards the person as a source of all values. Human values are found in experience, but person is seen as the only unifying principle of these experiences. Moreover, the contents of experiences are turned not so much towards existence, as towards their essence, and thus the phenomenology of Scheler can be defined as an essential personalism.

Although Karol Wojtyla appreciates the phenomenological description of person as based on human experience, he criticizes Scheler's personalism as lacking a proper metaphysical dimension, and for depriving human actions of any transcendental character, especially in the realm of ethical norms. From the metaphysical point of view, Wojtyla maintains that a human person must be regarded as a substantial being, because only as such can a person be the causative subject of his acts and efficient cause of all human values. Thus the very nature of human person is viewed as having an objective existence, and all his values, which are rooted in this objective existence, are directed beyond man's nature alone. Thus conceived, Wojtyla's anthropology can be called existential personalism.

---

[24] "Humanism a cel czlowieka," in: "Aby Chrystus sie nami poslugiwal" (Kraków: *Znak*, 1979), p. 149.

[25] *Ocena mozliwosci zbudowania etyki chrzescijanskiej przy zalozeniach systemu Maksa Schelera* (Lublin: Towarzystwo Naukowe KUL, 1959), p. 135.

It will suffice for our purpose to limit our quest for existence without entering into the whole problematics of the meaning of existence[26] by asking how existence expresses any particular thing in its very nature. Generally speaking, any particular thing is posited in its nature as something which brings it into existence through which it is expressed as present in reality. In other words, although existence does not predicate anything about the nature as such, and therefore it cannot give any knowledge of the essence of the thing, nevertheless, by existence, a thing is posited in its nature as being really real in reality, and it expresses not the how' of the nature of the thing, but 'that' which it is in reality. However, if existence means only the presentness of things as being posited in their own nature in reality, then, by the same token, it allows us to pursue the question of how things can fulfill their nature in reality, namely the way of realization of their own perfection. In the order of all created things there are, according to St. Thomas, two kinds of perfection, namely immanent and transcendent. The immanent perfection of all created things consists in a twofold goodness: the goodness of the universe as a whole, and the goodness of the intellectual nature. The transcendent perfection of the order of the universe is that which is *propinquissimum* in creatures to the divine goodness.[27]

In the order of the universe, natural things tend to participate in divine goodness as in their ultimate end according to their proper nature. But because man has not only a material but also an intellectual nature, he belongs to the highest rank in the universe,[28] "intellectual natures have a closer relationship to a whole than other natures."[29] The main task of St. Thomas's philosophical anthropology so understood

---

[26] Cf. Joseph Owens, *An Interpretation of Existence* (Milwaukee: The Bruce Publishing Company, 1968).
[27] *SCG*, III, 64.
[28] *Ibid.*, III, 120.
[29] *Ibid.*, II, 23.

is, therefore, to discover the proper place which man occupies in the order of nature, to reflect this order in the human soul, and to find the divine intention in creating the world for man. In the words of St. Thomas: "This then is the ultimate perfection to which, according to philosophers, a human soul can arrive, namely, that in it the whole order of the universe can be described with all its causes. In this also all men find their ultimate end, which, according to us (sc. theologians) will be realized in the vision of God."[30]

In St. Thomas's philosophical anthropology man is very rarely treated as *persona*; as a matter of fact, the term itself is hardly mentioned in connection with human nature. According to Wojtyla, the problematic of person in St. Thomas is, above all, theological and not philosophical. Wojtyla remarks: "(In St. Thomas's) system person fulfills rather a theological function. In Christian thought theological personalism comes before humanistic personalism, as one can also easily observe in St. Thomas. Thus we encounter the word *persona* mainly in the treatises on the Holy Trinity and Incarnation, and it almost never appears in treatises on man."[31]

The chief reason why St. Thomas does not analyze man as a person lies in the fact that the Angelic Doctor also applies hylomorphism to his explanation of man. However, although hylomorphism is a universal theory which explains the structure and composition of natural things, it is insufficient and inadequate when applied to a full understanding of man in the transcending actions of his intellect and will. In the words of Wojtyla, hylomorphism explains only "*compositum humanum*; in the first place, it profoundly analyzes the human soul which plays the role of a substantial form in that *compositum*,"[32] and in this way it stresses the unity of man only.

---

[30] *De Veritate*, 2, 2c.
[31] "Personalism tomistyczny," *Znak*, p. 665.
[32] *Ibid.*, p. 667.

Realizing the insufficiency of trying to understand human nature in its entirety by hylomorphic doctrine alone, St. Thomas saw in the human soul not only a substantial form of a body, but he also gave to "the operations of understanding and will"[33] a separate subsistent form with its own *esse*, which is independent of that of the whole composition. Wojtyla sought to improve on this double standard of the human soul. This he did by integrating human nature. He writes:

> We see clearly enough that the integration of nature by the person in the human being not only presupposes humanness, but it also derives its real constitution from it. Hence, no other nature has any real (that is, individual) existence as a person--for this pertains to man alone."[34]

III

The principle which states that only human nature has "existence as a person" enables Wojtyla not only to avoid the double standard of human soul, but to build his philosophical anthropology on such a form of personalism which will identify and integrate man's nature with his human existence. In other words, without denying the validity of hylomorphism, Wojtyla's personalism points out that in opposition to other things, human nature is posited in its existence not only as an individual substance, but above all as a personal subject of its own existence and actions: "Man is an individual (*individua substantia*) of a rational nature. The rational nature does not possess its own subsistence as a nature, but subsists in a person. Person, therefore, is the subsistent

---

[33] *SCG*, II, 81.
[34] *Osoba i czyn* (Kraków: Polskie Towarzystwo Teologiczne, 1985), p. 107.

subject of existence and actions, which cannot be in any way attributed to rational nature."[35]

But, if man has "existence as a person," then the question arises: how is human nature expressed in its reality? Answering this question Wojtyla points to specific character of man, namely, the dynamization of his subject:

> Dynamization by the personal being must lie at the roots of the integration of humanness by the person. At any rate, considering this experiential cohesion of the whole human functioning with his existence, we are led to accept that it is human nature that constitutes the appropriate basis for the cohesion of the man-subject—whatever kind of inner dynamism it has-- with any of its dynamization; of course, nature as the basis of this dynamic cohesion really inheres in the subject, while the subject itself, having personal existence, is a person.[36]

Dynamization of man's subjectivity causes that "the person becomes the object of his own actions."[37] In other words, in opposition to all other natural things, man conceived as a person with dynamization of his subjectivity is a being *sui generis*, and his nature is identified with existence. Viewing man in his existential dimensions as person is in accord with the whole Judeo-Christian tradition of understanding both *humanum* and *divinum*.

Limiting ourselves to the earliest period of Judeo-Christian tradition, we can see that the predominant tendency in resolving the question of human reality is to describe man in terms of his existence rather than to give some specific definition to the essential characteristics of his nature. The Jewish philosopher, Philon of Alexandria, had already given, in the first century of our era, an existential interpretation of man. The name 'Jahveh' Philon translates as "I am who I am" (*ego eimi ho on*), and designates the human condition as man

---

[35] "Personalism tomistyczny", *Znak*, p. 666.
[36] *Osoba i czyn*, p. 106.
[37] *Ibid.*, p. 252.

merging with God, for "only God consists in being pure existence" (*ho theos monos en to einai hyphesteken*).[38] In the same vein St. Jerome translates God's name in Exodus 3:14 as existence (*ego sum qui sum*). But, since man is created according to God's image, then his destiny is also to live as an existing being which is realized in becoming God. Consequently, through existence man is different from the essence of other creatures, as expressed by St. Gregory: "by essence man is different from horse, but by *hypostasis* Peter is different from Paul."[39] According to Teodoretus of Cypres, 'essence' (*ousia*) designates "that which is" (*to ti einai*), and *'hypostasis'* means existence (*to einai*).[40] This terminology becomes more precisely formulated by Anicius Marcus Severinus Boethius (480-525) who gave us the famous classical definition of person as "individual substance of rational nature"--"*persona est naturae rationalis individua substantia.*"[41]

In the following ages, the Boethian definition of person as an individual substance of a rational nature had been usually interpreted in the spirit of Aristotelian doctrine on nature. This tendency toward Aristotelian naturalism can also be detected in St. Thomas's interpretation of person. When interpreting Boethius's definition of person, St. Thomas writes: "the definition of person contains individual substance in so far as it signifies singularity in rational substances."[42] And even if Aquinas seems to weaken the character of individual substantiality of person he, nonetheless, stresses the essential perspectives of person in the *humanum*: "the name *persona* is not meant to

---

[38] *Philonis Alexandrini Opera Quae supersunt* (Berolini: Georgii Reimeri, MDCCCLXXXXVI): vol. I, p. 294, 20.

[39] *S.P.N. Gregorii Episcopi Nysseni Opera Omnia quae reperiri potuerunt omnia*, in: *Patrologia Graeca*, 45, col. 184.

[40] *Theodoreti Cyrensis Episcopi Opera Omnia* in: *Patrologia Graeca*, 83, col. 33.

[41] *Manlii Severini Boetii Opera Omnia*, in: *Patrologia Latina*, 64, col. 1343.

[42] *S.th.*, I, 29, 1c; cf. Pot., 9, 2c; ad 7; Sent., I, 29, 1, 1c; II, 3, 1, 2c.

signify individualness from nature itself (*individuum ex parte naturae*) but it signifies things which subsist in such a nature."⁴³ Moreover, when identifying *persona* with *hypostasis* Aquinas considers person in terms of a complete nature of all species: "not any one particular substance is *hypostasis*, or person, but this which possesses the complete nature of species."⁴⁴ Person then is the highest perfection in the whole nature, by "adding to the very essence (*rationem essentiae*) individual principles."⁴⁵ When he discusses the dignity of man, the Angelic Doctor attributes the subsistence of man to rational nature: "and since the greatness of dignity is subsisting in rational nature, then any individual thing of rational nature is called a person."⁴⁶

Under the influence of Max Scheler, Karol Wojtyla challenged the classical understanding of Boethius's definition of person and searched for a new approach in defining man as a person. Again Wojtyla agrees with Boethius and St. Thomas that person is both, *individua substantia* and *suppositum*, but "the concept of the 'person' is broader than the concept of the 'individual,' just as the person is more than individualized nature."⁴⁷ Even if our author accepts Boethius's definition of person, nevertheless "in our perspective it seems clear that neither the concept of the 'rational nature' nor that of its individualization seems to express fully the specific completeness expressed by the concept of the person. The completeness we are speaking of here seems to be something that is unique in a very special sense rather than concrete. In everyday use we may substitute for a person straightforward 'somebody'...(which) reaches to the very roots of the being that

---

43 *S.th.*, 1, 30, 4c.
44 *Ibid.*, I, 75, 4 ad 2; cf. III, 2, 2 ad 3; 3, 1 ad 2; SCG, IV, 10; 35; 38; 41.
45 *S.th.*, I, 29, 2 ad 3.
46 *Ibid.*, I, 29, 3 ad 2; cf. *Pot.*, 8, 4 ad 5.
47 *Osoba i Czyn*, p. 95.

is the subject."⁴⁸ This completeness which is unique to man as a person results in a specific dialectical process of self experiencing: "he is both the actor and the subject, and he has experience of himself as actor and as a subject, though the experience which he has of his efficacy is overshadowed by the experience of his subjectiveness."⁴⁹

Christian humanism re-analyzed in the light of Karol Wojtyla's personalism received a new existential interpretation. In poetic expression the Bishop of Kraków, writing under his *nom de plume* Andrzej Jawien, described the existential personalism of Christian humanism in such a way that each human person "has at his disposal some kind of existence, and some kind of love." The question remains: "how can a sensible unity be made of these?"⁵⁰ The Christian humanism, then, consists in finding a way of resolving human existence through love. As Bishop of Kraków, Karol Wojtyla held that the resolution of human existence is found in "a harmony between truth and freedom." As Bishop of Rome, the same Karol Wojtyla told the General Audience on July 14, 1983, that there is in human existence an essential "connection between truth and freedom."⁵¹

Christian humanism as viewed by the then Karol Wojtyla and the present John Paul II is based on two sets of human values: a synthesis of existence and love, and a connection between truth and freedom. Based on these two sets of human values, our author lays down a new foundation for Christian ethics. On the one hand, Christian ethics, based on Wojtyla's existential personalism, is fulfilling the requirements of "naturalistic" humanism, because it takes into account both the

---

48 *Ibid.*
49 *Ibid.*, p. 97.
50 "Przed sklepem jubilera," *Znak*, 12 (1960), p. 1605f.
51 "Christian ethics based on harmony between truth and freedom," *L'Osservatore Romano*, July 18, 1983.

individual experience and personal freedom of man. In the words of John Paul II: "to speak of 'ethos' means to recall an experience that every man, not only the Christian, lives daily: it is at the same time simple and complex, profound and elementary. This experience is always connected with that of his own <u>freedom,</u> that is, the fact that each one of us is truly and really the <u>cause of his/her own acts.</u>"[52] On the other hand, an ethical system which stems from Wojtyla's existential personalism is grounded in one's own experience of *divinum*: "In the ethical experience, therefore, there is established a <u>connection between truth and freedom,</u> thanks to which the person becomes evermore himself, in obedience to the creative wisdom of God."[53]

IV

The main theme of his first encyclical "Redemptor Hominis" was described by John Paul II on March 11, 1979, during his speech before *Angelus,* as follows: "...as I see and sense the relationship between the mystery of Redemption and the dignity of man, I also desire to unify the mission of the Church with the service to man in his unfathomed mystery."[54] Earlier, on December 2, 1978, John Paul II at the United Nations, when asked by Secretary General Kurt Waldheim, "what basis can we offer as the soil in which individual and social rights might grow?" answered: "Unquestionably that basis is the dignity of the human person."[55] To properly

---

[52] *Ibid.*
[53] *Ibid.*
[54] From now on, quotation from Redemptor Hominis will be followed by number referring to the division in the text.. "Ze Stolicy Piotrowej," *Tygodnik Powszechny*, 13 (1979).
[55] "Papal Message on Human Rights to the United Nations", *Pope John Paul II Center Newsletter*, v. 1, No. 1, January-February 1979, p. 7.

understand the specific dignity of man as a person, we must, therefore, raise very profound questions on man's unique quality of his nature: Is there in man any specific characteristic which would permit us to treat him as a more worthy creature than any other being in the universe? What kind of importance can man find in himself that would justify his being a higher being than anything else? In other words: what makes man different from other beings?

To answer these questions one must search for a specific value which enables man not only to be a more precious creature, but to be indispensible both as irrepeatable and irreplaceable in his/her own unique individual existence. John Paul II, referring to St. Thomas's doctrine on values, says that the human existence of each and every individual man reveals his dignity in/through love; in "Redemptor Hominis" we read:

> Above all, Love is greater than sin, than weakness, than the vanity of creation, it is stronger than death; it is a Love always ready to raise up and forgive; always ready to go to meet the prodigal son; always looking for 'the revealing of the sons of God' who are called to the glory, that is to be revealed. (II, 9)

The very nature of human dignity consists in the fact that man's existence is not a ready-made entity, but that man is a creature which has to fulfil himself as the "most important point of the visible world" (II, 8), and to complete thus the *opus creationis* by his/her own actions of constant loving. Referring to the Church's mission, John Paul II calls love the source "in all humanity's various spheres of existence" (I, 4). In more simple words, human dignity consists in "penetrating like Christ the depth of human conscience, by touching the inner mystery of man which in biblical and non-biblical language is expressed by the word 'heart'" (II,8). But, since the human dignity of man's existence reached its highest point of Love in Christ, "The Redeemer of the World (He is the One) who penetrated in a unique and unrepeatable way into the mystery of man and entered his 'heart'" (II, 8).

Proclaiming love as the ultimate source of human dignity, John Paul II grounds Christian humanism on the principle of preservation of the proper balance between man and nature. In "Redemptor Hominis", John Paul II, referring to the participation of man in the *munus regale* of Christ himself says:

> The essential meaning of this 'kingship' and 'dominion' of man over the visible world, which the Creator himself gave to man for his task, consists in the priority of ethics over technology, in the primacy of the person over things and in the superiority of spirit over matter. (III, 16)

Analyzing Christian humanism as viewed by the Pope in terms of this threefold priority of man over nature, enables one to evaluate his philosophico-theological anthropology as including and being based upon the following three principles: the principle of "having more" and "being more", the principle of participation and alienation, and finally the principle of human freedom and conscience.

V

Pointing to the fact of overdevelopment of the contemporary technology (II, 8), John Paul II warns that to the degree that man endangers the natural environment he loses his own dignity and undergoes a process of profound dehumanization (III.15). The main reason for this process of dehumanization of contemporary man "lies in an inadequate view of man",[56] and in treating the *humanum* without relating him to the *divinum*. In his paper delivered at the Catholic University of Milano on March 18, 1977, Cardinal Wojtyla stated:

---

[56] Address of John Paul II to the third assembly of Latin American bishops at Puebla, Mexico on January 28, 1978, *Acta Apostolicae Sedis*, 71 (1971), 1.9. Cf. also "Humanizm a cel czlowieka", *Tygodnik Powszechny*, 31 (1957).

This is not only a controversy inside the Church or in Christianity, or even within the orbit of non-Christian religions. This is, above all, a controversy with atheism which more often denies the *divinum* in the name of *humanum*. Atheism in the form of Marxism denies referring to God- Creator as a way of constituting the human person, it means, the image of God, and establishes with the *humanum* the collective form of existence as the foundation and final existence at the same time. In this historical context the category of 'persona' which <u>must be a fundamental idea in the controversy about the *humanum*</u> is essentially a Christian one."[57]

In resolving this controversy between theistic and atheistic humanisms we have to view man's dignity as an individual "autonomous subject"[58] and by the same token reject the Marxian concept of man as a species-being (*Gattungswesen*), on one hand, and properly estimate the priority of man in his human *praxis*, on the other hand.

Referring to human *praxis*, Wojtyla distinguishes in man a twofold aspect of his actions through which an individual person reveals himself, namely 'transitive' and 'non-transitive':

According to my opinion, founded on St. Thomas Aquinas, the human act, that is the act which is simultaneously 'transitive' (*transiens*) and 'non-transitive' (*non-transiens*). It is transitive inasmuch as it goes to the other side of the subject, seeking an expression or an effect in the external world, and thus objectivizes itself in some product. It is non transitive in the measure in which 'remaining in the subject' in which it determines the quality and the value, and establishes his own *'fieri'* essentially human. Therefore man, acting not only fulfills some actions, but in some way realizes himself and becomes himself.[59]

In view of this twofold aspect of human action as being both transitive and non-transitive, Wojtyla proclaims "the priority

---

[57] "Il problema del costituirsi della cultura attraverso la 'praxis' umana", *Rivista di filosofia neo-scholastica*, 49 (1977), fasc. 3, p. 515.

[58] *Ibid.*, p. 516. Cf. "Wartosci", *Tygodnik Powszechny* 39 (1957).

[59] "Il problema", *Rivista di filosofia neo-scholastica*.

of man as a subject of the act as having a fundamental significance for the forming of culture through human *praxis*."[60]

Properly understood priority of man over nature consists in finding a proper balance between transitive and non-transitive aspects of our activity. In this respect Cardinal Wojtyla comes to the conclusion that "the intransitive is then more important than that which is transitive, which is objectivized in some product and which serves the transformation of the world or its exploitation; otherwise man would be subjected to frustration."[61]

To avoid man's frustration over his own product, Wojtyla, referring to the French philosopher Gabriel Marcel's distinction between 'having' and 'being', proclaims that the priority of intransitive characteristic of man as a person over/against the transitive one leads to the acceptance of the postulate as a categorical imperative, that it is more important of "being more" than "having more" (II, 16).

In view of this twofold aspect of human actions as both transitive and non-transitive and the postulate of "being more" rather than "having more", John Paul II proclaims the priority of ethics over things and technology. In his own words: "The development of technology and the development of contemporary civilization which marked by the domination of technology, demand a proportional development of morals and ethics" (III, 15).

VI

Human dignity must base itself on self-respect of one's own self and the respect for other fellow men. The reason for such a

---

[60] *Ibid.*
[61] *Ibid.*, p. 518. Cf. also "Teoria e prassi nella filosofia della persona umana", *Sapienza*, 4 (1976), pp. 377- 384.

respect consists, according to John Paul, in "a feeling of deep esteem for 'what is in man', for what man himself worked out in the depths of his spirit concerning that most profound and important problem of respecting everything that has been brought about in him by the Spirit which 'blows where he wills'" (II, 12). Cultivating this "feeling of deep esteem" for each and every human person is the cornerstone of building any communal life of all men, which Card. Wojtyla described as participation in terms of a relation of man to man.[62]

In view of the mutual relation between man and man, participation in humanity is based on mutual primacy of 'I' in regard to each other, as being regarded as person, constituting thus communal ties which are always secondary to the personal one. In other words, the mutual participation of 'I' in the other person is by the same token indicative of the primacy of personal subjects over the community.

The principle of participation so conceived is not always a reality, and as such it is endangered by a real process of alienating of man from each other. Referring to the existing socio-economic situation of the contemporary world, John Paul II writes:

> The man of today seems ever to be under threat from what he produces, that is to say from the result of the work of his hands and, even more so, of the work of his intellect and the tendencies of his will. All too soon, and often in an unforeseeable way, what this manifold activity of man yields is not only subjected to 'alienation', in the sense that it is simply taken away from the person who produces it, but rather it turns against man himself, at least in part, through the indirect consequences of its effects returning on himself. It is or can be directed against him. This seems to make up the main chapter of the drama of present-day human existence in its broadest and universal dimension (III, 15).

---

[62] Cf. "Osoba: podmiot i wspotnota". *Roczniki Filozoficzne*, 2 (1976), pp. 5-39.

The result of alienation is an existential fear of losing human dignity:

> He is afraid that what he produces—not all of it, of course, or even most of it, but part of it and precisely that part that contains a special share of his genius and initiative--can radically turn against himself; he is afraid that it can become the means and instrument for an unimaginable self-destruction, compared with which all the cataclysms and catastrophes of history known to us seem to fade away (III, 15).

Now, the process of alienation of man can be overcome by developing among people the spirit of solidarity (III, 16). The spirit of solidarity will lead, according to our Pope, not only to "a true conversion of mind, will and heart", but also to building "a road of the necessary transformation of the structures of economic life" and social justice (III, 16). The principle of solidarity is not, however, a fact but a task which "requires resolute involvement by individuals and peoples that are free and united." (III, 16) Appealing to "the deepest powers in man, which decide the true culture of peoples", John Paul II believes that "such involvement of people will express man's true freedom...." (III, 16).

VII

Individual human being analyzed in his human dignity constitutes a specific process of 'self-determination' through which man becomes a person by his actions.[63] 'Self-determination', however, reveals two aspects of a person:

1) 'self-possession' (*persona est sui iuris*), and
2) 'self-domination' (*persona est dominus sui*),

---

[63] Cf. "The Structure of Self-Determination at the Core of the Theory of the Person", in *Congresso Internazionale Tomasso D'Aquino nel suo Settimo Centenario* (Rome/Naples, 1974), pp. 37-44.

'Self-determination' reveals in person 'self-possession': "'I want' as an actual self-determination establishes structural self-possession. One can only decide about that which one possesses in reality. Man himself decides about himself through his own will, since he possesses himself."[64] 'Self-possession', however, points only to the passive character of 'self-determination' of that what 'I want' and it is only a condition for actual realization of my 'wants' by my will, namely, 'self- domination': "here the person is someone who dominates and controls himself, on one hand, and he is someone over whom he himself has domination."[65] This twofold aspect of 'self-determination' of man reveals a person not only for what someone is, but also for who one is: "Making his own 'I' as somebody, man at the same time becomes some-one."[66] In this way the twofold aspect of 'self-determination' of 'man- person' points to human freedom. Analyzing human freedom in terms of 'self- determination', Wojtyla concludes that this characteristic of man, who through his actions can give himself a direction, indicates that man's will is endowed with transcendent perspectives. Referring to *Gaudium et Spes* the Pope says: "In the name of this solicitude (sc. of Christ) as we read in the council's pastoral constitution, 'the church must in no way be confused with the political community, nor bound to any political system. She is at once a sign and a safeguard of the transcendence of the human person.'" (III, 13). Freedom, however, as the basic principle of human actions understood in terms of transcendent self-determination of each and every human person, is not absolute. In this respect, our Pope warns us:

> Nowadays it is sometimes held, though wrongfully, that freedom is an end in itself, that each human being is free when he makes use of freedom as he wishes, and that this must be our aim in the lives of individuals and societies. In reality, freedom is a great gift

---

[64] *Osoba i Czyn*, p. 132.
[65] *Ibid.*, p. 133.
[66] *Ibid.*, p. 136.

only when we know how to use it consciously for everything that is our true good (IV, 21).

The question arises: what is the criterion of an authentic use of our freedom? In what way can man determine himself as such? How can a person reveal his own true self through his actions? In other words, where is the ultimate source of the human transcendent freedom?

As an ethician, Cardinal Wojtyla searched for the criteria of human freedom in the moral behavior of man, as the most sensitive and "visible" test of man's dignity which consists in searching for his own goodness, and which *Redemptor Hominis* grounds on conscience (II, 12).

Individual human conscience is the final and deepest root of morality in/through which man determines himself through actions and reveals his own dignity in the most profound way: "Conscience as a key-point of that personal 'self-completion' of the subject points, in a significant manner, to transcendence, remaining, so to speak, in its very subjective core."[67] Without going into details, I shall simply summarize the role of conscience in man's 'self-completion' in the words of Wojtyla:

> There exists a correlation between conscience as the inner-personal source of duty and the objective order of moral norms... The basic value of the norms lies in the truth of good, which is objectified in them, and not in duty itself, although the normative words used in the given cases accentuate duty, having recourse to such phrases as 'one should', 'one ought to', 'the obligation exists' and the like. The essence of normative opinions of morality or right is inherent all the more considerably in the truth of good, which is objectivized in them. Through this truth they obtain contact with the conscience, which to some extent transforms this truth into concrete and real obligation.[68]

---

[67] "Osoba: podmiot i wspolnota", *Roczniki Filozoficzne*, p. 18.
[68] *Osoba i Czyn*, p. 199.

VII. ON HUMAN BEING AS PERSON

Man has been defined in many ways. Since he has various attributes and different qualities, Man is called *homo divinus* and *homo religiosus, homo spiritus,* and *homo sapiens, homo faber* and *homo oeconomicus, homo ludens* and *homo loquans, Grand Etre* and *l'homme deprave, l'homme libre* and *l'homme revolte, l'homme inconnu* and *l'homme machine,* a symbol-making creature and a tool-making animal, a horde animal and... On the enormous listings of descriptions of man, many of them omit references to the bodily factor in defining human nature. In such definitions the absence of somatic elements of man (which is so prevalent in all kinds of materialistic and empiricist systems) is perhaps caused by the influence of

Platonic idea of soul as a supreme and essential property of man which is using body only as a means for self-liberation.[1]

I

To avoid the Platonic dualistic view of man in which human body is suppressed to the demands of being only a tool for soul, Wojtyla is choosing *homo Aristotelicus* which does not "isolate the body and its role in the dynamic whole of both person and act."[2] On the contrary, in the Aristotelian anthropology there is enough room to treat man as a person who integrates both body and soul without opposing them against each other. Referring to the integrity of person and his actions, Wojtyla accepts the duality of man's nature as a composition of body and soul:

> Integration--precisely because it is the complementary aspect of the transcendence of the person in the action--tells us that the soul/body relation cuts across all the boundaries we find in experience and that it goes deeper and in more fundamental than they are. And perhaps in this depends indirectly the verification of the truth that both the reality of soul and its relation to body can be properly expressed only in metaphysical categories."[3]

Wojtyla concludes that the paradigm of soul and body in man can best be explained by the Aristotelico-Thomistic hylomorphism:

> In this respect it is most appropriate to fully accept the view of the human reality, which we received from traditional philosophy (Aristotle, Thomas Aquinas), thus discovering in it alongside of the 'material-hyle' element also the element of *'forma-morphe'*.

---

[1] Cf. *De Platonis doctrina circa animam. Textus et documenta*, ed. by J. Souilhe (Romae: Pontificia Universitas Gregoriana, 1932), p. 16.

[2] *Osoba i czyn* (Kraków: Polskie Towarzystwo Teologiczne, 1985), p. 249.

[3] *Ibid.*, p. 319.

> Consequently, the theory of hylomorphism and the analysis of man carried out within its frame...[4]

Unfortunately, in the past, hylomorphism received different interpretations. St. Thomas detects two main misinterpretations which endanger the proper understanding of Aristotelian hylomorphism, namely:

1) a misinterpretation which usually is caused by an inappropriate understanding of prime matter as some potentiality;

2) a misinterpretation which is caused by improper understanding of substantial form as some actuality. The former leads to the doctrine of duplicity of matter and the latter to the theory of multiplicity of substantial forms in particular created beings. A typical example of these misinterpretations of the Aristotelian theory of act and potency, a misinterpretation which already occurred in the Middle Ages, was that of panhylomorphism.[5]

St. Thomas rejected totally the panhylomorphism of Avencebrol and he calls the proposition of *binarium famosissimum* a frivolous and impossible solution."[6] In view of St. Thomas, the primary error of panhylomorphism consists in identifying the potentiality which occurs in material being with the potentiality which appears in spiritual beings. Moreover, panhylomorphism contains also an erroneous postulate of the existence of multiplicity of forms by which being is established in its genus and species. St. Thomas's solution is that we must distinguish between substantial and accidental forms, and that in every being apart from many accidental forms there can be but one substantial form.

---

[4] *Ibid.*, p. 249.

[5] The originator of panhylomorphism was Avencebrol, cf. *Fons Vitae*, in *Beiträge zur Geschichte der Philosophie des Mittelalters*, I, 2-4 (Münster, 1892-1895). Cf. also M. Wittman, *Die Stellung des hl. Thomas von Aquin zu Avencebrol*, in: *Beiträge zur Geschichte der Philosophie des Mittelalters*, III, 2 (Münster, 1900).

[6] *An.*, 6, 4c.

St. Thomas not only rejected panhylomorphism in general, but he specifically avoids it in his anthropology. St. Thomas interprets his hylomorphic anthropology existentially in regard to human composition. In his very first work, *De Ente et Essentia*, the Angelic Doctor writes: "*A quibusdam dicuntur huiusmodi substantiae compositae ex quo est et quod est vel ex quod est et esse ut Boethius dicit.*"[7] ("A substance of this kind [sc. spiritual] is composed of that by which it is and that which it is, or, as Boethius says, of that which it is and its act of existing.") Moreover, St. Thomas introduces a term '*subsistentia*' which he applies to human existence.[8]

Wojtyla accepts the Aristotelian hylomorphism but as interpreted by St. Thomas and applies its principles to his personalistic anthropology.[9] In *Osoba i Czyn*, Wojtyla accepts the doctrines of St. Thomas on

1) the composition of soul and body;[10]

2) the theory of analogy of being as applied to the dynamic unity of actuality and potentiality,[11]

3) the understanding of *esse et fieri* in terms of causality,[12]

4) the hylomorphism of Aristotle and St. Thomas,[13]

5) the theory of man as *suppositum*, especially in relation to St. Thomas's understanding of *esse*,[14]

6) the ontological priority of being over action in man,[15]

---

[7] P. 17; Marietti.
[8] *SCG*, II, 57; 1334.
[9] Cf. "Osoba-Podmiot i wspolnota", *Roczniki Filozoficzne*, 2 (1976), f. 4, p. 7.
[10] Pp. 225ff.
[11] 82f.
[12] Pp. 69, 104ff.
[13] P. 226.
[14] P. 92.
[15] Passim.

7) the Boethian conception of man as a person but understood in terms of St. Thomas's teaching on *subsistentia* and *suppositum*,[16] and basing his theory of 'man/person' on the classical principles such as "*operari sequitur esse*", "*praxis sequitur theoriam*" etc.[17]

Moreover, Wojtyla is including the classical methods in the description of man, especially induction and reduction,[18] analogical reasoning[19] and causality.[20] Consequently, Wojtyla is also using the Thomistic terminology *actus-potentia, actus humanus et hominis, agere et pati*, etc.[21]

On the other hand, however, Wojtyla has some reservations about St. Thomas's doctrine on man, and he realizes certain objections as to the proper way of reconciling Boethius's definition of person with Aquinas's hylomorphic anthropology. Wojtyla accuses St. Thomas of using the term 'person' almost exclusively in the theological doctrine on Trinity and Incarnation, but never in philosophical anthropology. In the words of Wojtyla: "in his (sc. St. Thomas's) system, person complies with theological function.... Consequently we encounter the word 'person' in the treatises on Trinity and Incarnation, and it is hardly to be found in the works on man."[22]

However, Boethius encounters also some difficulties with his definition of person. In trying to solve the theological question of the duality of nature in Christ, Boethius's main objective in defining person was to establish properly the distinction between nature and person:

---

[16] Pp. 94ff.
[17] Passim.
[18] Pp. 19-22.
[19] Pp. 85, 124.
[20] Pp. 86ff.
[21] Passim.
[22] "Personalizm Tomistyczny", *Znak*, 5 (1961), p. 665.

> Many doubts arise when we speak of person, namely, which definition should be applied. If each nature has its person, then the issue remains unsolved, because what is the distinction between nature and person? If, on the other hand, person is not the same as nature, but exists within the limits and realm of nature, then it is difficult to say, to what kind of being 'person' can belong, that is, which being can possess person, and to which one the term 'person' applies[23].

Boethius realizes that the difficult problem of establishing the distinction between nature and person, and consequently defining properly the term 'person' is the concept of substance: "This was necessary in order to make evident the distinction between nature and person, namely, *'ousia'* and *'hyposthasis;'* however, where and how to use each of them, remains an ecclesiastical problem,... because nature is a determined specific property of substance."[24] As a result of contrasting nature and person in terms of substance, Boethius thought that he had arrived at a proper definition of person: "If then, person is to be found in substances, and at that in rational substances only, and every substance is nature, and /this nature/ is not found in universal things, but in individual ones, then we already have a definition of person: a person is an individual substance of rational nature."[25]

II

In order better to understand the Boethian definition of person, his followers investigated the relationship of the person and human reality, and they asked how the proposed definition of person applied in the philosophical anthropology. Accepting Aristotelian hylomorphism St. Thomas was convinced that

---

23 *De persona et duabus naturis*, Patrologia Latina, 64, c. 1342.
24 *Ibid.*, c. 1345.
25 *Ibid.*, c. 1343.

person can be applied to human nature in view of the composition of body and soul. And since a soul is *actus primus corporis physici organici potentia vitam habentis,* then human soul is the intellectual substance as a subsistent form of human rational nature. Man's intellectual substance is a form of body, but not in regard to his intellectual powers, because man's soul exists through its own *esse*, and not through *esse* of the whole composite. Man's soul exists through its own *esse*, because it is the principle of knowing and willing. In order to prove his solution, St. Thomas analyzes the modes of understanding (*intelligere*).

Understanding is the property of a soul and it is exercised in many different ways. As an intellectual substance, man performs two operations, namely, that of the soul and that of the whole composite. The operation of the soul needs the body only as an object. The operation of the whole composite needs body not only as an object but also as an instrument. The operation of the soul needs a body only as an object while the power through which it exercises itself belongs to soul itself. Consequently man's soul is an intellectual subsistent form.

Wojtyla does not deny the objectivity of St. Thomas's solution of *compositum humanum,* and he concludes that the Angelic Doctor applies the function of person to human rational soul. Referring to St. Thomas's teaching that man's soul is the substantial form in human composition, Wojtyla states:

> It is exactly the rational soul--*anima rationalis* (which is) the principle and source of the whole spirituality of man, and therefore also the proper title of conferring (on man's soul) the character of person."[26]

But, if person is the character of human soul, then what is the essential element which constitutes man as a person? Following St. Thomas, Wojtyla recognizes the ontological structure of person in *suppositum*. *Suppositum* is the key notion

---

[26] "Personalizm Tomistyczny", *Znak*, p. 667.

in properly understanding the Boethian definition of person. Wojtyla writes:

> In the first and fundamental approach the man/person has to be somewhat identified with *suppositum*. The person is a concrete man, the *individua substantia* of the classical Boethian definition. The concrete is in a way tantamount of the unique, or at any rate, to the individualized. The concept of the 'person' is broader and more comprehensive than the concept of the 'individual,' just as the person is more than individualized nature. The person would be an individual whose nature is rational—according to Boethius's full definition *persona est rationalis naturae individua substantia*.[27]

Since the *suppositum* is the ontological structure of a person, it consists of being some kind of a receptacle to be fulfilled. This fullness or completeness of man/person is-- according to Wojtyla--realized "neither in the concept of having the 'rational nature' nor in its individualization."[28] This completeness of person as being in its ontological structure a *suppositum*, Wojtyla recognizes in the dynamic character and transcendental nature of human actions through which man is always determining himself. Consequently, the constitutivum *personae* consists in self-determination which is the essential mark of each and every human being. In the words of Wojtyla: "The question of the personal structure of self-determination constitutes the very core of my work The Acting Person."[29]

Self-determination through actions Wojtyla understands as an ontic property of person and his freedom. Moreover, self-determination through his actions reveals that man as person can govern and possess himself. This self-governance and self-possession indicates that man experiences himself through his own actions as a personal subject. At this point, Wojtyla arrives

---

[27] *Osoba i czyn*, p. 95.

[28] *Ibid*.

[29] "The Structure of Self-Determination as the Core of the Theory of the Person," in: *Congresso Internazionale Tomasso D'Aquino nel suo Settimo Centenario* (Rome/Naples, 1974), p. 37.

to the definition of self-determination: "The first definition of self-determination in the experience of the human action includes the apprehension of being oneself the agency--the property of being the agent--of the personal self: 'I do' means that 'I am the efficient cause' of my action, of the actualization of myself as the subject."[30]

Self-determination understood as self-actualization of man's subjectivity shows that a person is transcendental in nature and dynamic in character. Self-determination indicates the transcendency of person, because experiencing one's own subjectivity as a self-agency transgresses the limitations of human nature as such according to the principle that the greater degree the actions the greater experience of oneself. Self-determination points also to the dynamism of person, because man is able to self-complete his being according to the principle that the higher the values of his actions, the higher his being. In the words of Wojtyla:

> The apprehension of the agency of the subject, that is active with regard to his own action, is strictly connected with his own action, is strictly connected with his apprehending the responsibility of his actions, which refers first of all to the axiological and ethical content of the action. All this forms, as if organically, a part of the experience of self-determination, but is revealed in it in different degrees. It depends, one may say, on the degree of personal 'maturity' of the action. The greater its degree of maturity, the more distinct becomes the experience of self-determination by the acting subject. The greater the consciousness of doing and the awareness of values, the more distinctly does man--the subject--experience self- determination. Thus, the more vivid his experience of it, the more clearly does he visualize in his experience and consciousness his own agency and responsibility.[31]

Self-determination, then, is the transcendental and dynamic property of man/person, and not of his will alone. In human will this property manifests its power in the personal

---

30 *Ibid.*, p. 38.
31 *Ibid.*, p. 39.

actions of choosing and decision. But if man realizes himself by self-determination in action, then the transcendental and dynamic property of the person's will points that man/person is an ontological unity in spirit which integrates the *compositum humanum* of body and soul, and makes it a transphenomenal and transexperiential entity.32 Comparing his view as man/person with the Boethian definition of person, Wojtyla writes:

> This analysis, however summary, allows us to see that self-determination is a particularity of person, of that person of whom the famous definition says, '*rationalis naturae substantia*'. This particularity is actualized by the will, which constitutes a power, an accidentality. Self-determination constitutes the essential factor of man's freedom. It is not only to the accidental aspect of the human being, but pertains to the 'substantial' aspect of the person: it is the freedom of the human being and not just the freedom of the will in man, though of course it is man's freedom which manifests itself by his will.33

However, if self-determination is not a property of the will but of the person understood as a transcendental entity with a dynamic nature, then self-determination cannot be understood "in the phenomenological terms of an intentional act."34 The intentional act of the will is only--according to Wojtyla--an aspect of a horizontal transcendency of the human actions. But the act of the will of man/person himself consists of vertical transcendency of human self-determination:

> The concept of self-determination contains more than the concept of agency: man not only performs his actions, but by his actions he becomes, in one way or another, his own 'maker'. Doing is accompanied by becoming; and, what is more, the two are organically fused together. This is the reason why self-determination, not only agency of the personal self alone,

---

32 In his conclusion Wojtyla's view in this regard is very close to that of S. Kierkegaard, cf. *The Sickness Unto Death* (Princeton: Princeton University Press, 1970), p. 146f.
33 "The Structure of Self-Determination", p. 40.
34 *Ibid*.

explains the reality and the personal nature of moral values—it explains the reality of the fact that by his action man becomes either 'good' or 'bad', and once he has become one or the other, it is as man that he is 'good' or 'bad'—according to St. Thomas' capital formula (Cf. e.g. Sth, I-II, 56, 3c). If we were to restrict the analysis of the will, conceived merely as an intentional act, and accept only the horizontal transcendence of the act, then this realism and the personal nature of moral values, of good and evil in man, would remain entirely unaccounted for.[35]

In summary we may say that intentionality is object-oriented, and self-determination is subject-oriented. In view of this distinction, Wojtyla overcomes not only the essentialist interpretation of person given by Max Scheler, but he also revises the traditional Thomistic hylomorphic anthropology by the concept of self-determination, understood, however, not as a simple act of the will but of the inner nature of person as such. We might conclude with the words of our author:

> It is not the question of the metaphysical complexity of the soul and body (*materia prima-- forma substantialis*), which is proper to man as a being, but of a complexity of a more phenomenological character. The phenomenological experience shows man as having himself possession of himself and at the same time being in the possession of himself. It also shows him as having control over himself and at the same time being controlled by himself. Both situations are revealed by self-determination, they are implied by it, and they also add wealth to the contents of self-determination. It is owing to self-possession and self-control that the personal structure of self-determination is so vividly exposed in its characteristic fullness.[36]

---

[35] *Ibid.*
[36] *Ibid.*, p. 42.

III

Searching for being of things, man realizes that he himself is an existing being. For man cannot attain the metaphysical truth about reality without having a consciousness of his own existence. The truth about reality and truth about man, therefore, is combined in a specific hermeneutical spiral: to understand man's self is the condition for understanding reality, and *vice versa*. The result of this hermeneutical spiral of human cognition is that the metaphysical understanding of being *qua* being, depends on philosophical understanding of man in his own existence. In a word, there is a dialectical complementarity between the metaphysical and the anthropological understanding of being of things.

However, since man can primarily reveal himself as an existing being only on account of his cognitive act of knowing external reality not from within but from without, then there must be the priority of metaphysical understanding of man over his anthropological existential examination. For man does not know himself and his inner world from the standpoint of a neutral observer, but he gets to know himself in actions. Man is simultaneously the observing, the communicating and the acting being which is both physical and spiritual. My consciousness penetrates into the movements and reactions of my body which only in a specific sense is something "eternal". But, as an acting being, man manifests himself as a subject from which all his actions emerge.

In this classical metaphysics, however, man as an acting subject has been understood as a natural *suppositum*, i.e., as a substantial form of body. This conception of man as a natural subject of all his actions, deprives man from being conscious of his own existence as somebody who could be able to say about himself "I am". But, in fact man is conscious of his own unrepeatable and unique existence which constitutes his very own identity by which he can say "I exist" as my own self.

Therefore, man as a self-identified existing "I" who is conscious of his own existence cannot be treated simply as a part of nature, i.e., as a natural subject which could be defined as some individual among other beings, belonging simply to the same genus.

This view on man as a self-identified existing "I" who can be conscious of his unique and unrepeatable act of existing subject of all his actions, is the point of departure of the Lublin Thomists from that of the Catholic French existentialists. In co-operation with the metaphysical speculation of Krapiec and the historical investigation of Swiezawski (both from the Catholic University of Lublin (Poland)), Karol Wojtyla sought the existential identity of man not in the natural, but rather personal subjectivity of human self.[37] Viewing man as an agent who experiences his own existence in both the immanent and the transcendental order of his human nature, Wojtyla lays the foundation for a new version of St. Thomas's doctrine on man; Wojtyla's synthesis has been described as "existential personalism".[38]

At the base of Wojtyla's existential personalism lies the fact that man finds himself in a permanent state of experiencing his existence. As a matter of fact, although I do not know what I am in my inner contentless structure, I am always conscious of my existence which is for me a constant source of all my actions. But, experiencing my "I" as existing in all my actions, I experience my being from within, and in this way I attest to the primacy of my existence of my being through actions. In conclusion Wojtyla says: "Actions are particular moments in my self-inspection (*oglad*) an experiential cognition

---

[37] *Osoba i czyn.*
[38] Cf. Andrew N. Woznicki, *A Christian Humanism: Karol Wojtyla's Existential Personalism* (New Britain: Mariel Publications, 1983).

of a person. Actions, therefore, constitute the most proper starting point for understanding man in his dynamic nature."[39]

Wojtyla, in the evaluation of man's existence, uses experience as his starting point, and he sees experience as a basic characteristic of man as a being who constitutes himself as a person through his actions. Wojtyla goes on to accept consciousness as *residuum* of self-cognition through which each individual man constitutes himself as a human being. For Wojtyla, however, human consciousness in its very core is devoid of pure intentionality, but rather it is endowed with a twofold foundation: reflectiveness and reflexiveness; in the former consciousness plays the role of human objective cognition (and this "cognitive" consciousness consists of intentionality but understood as in the classical philosophy), and in the latter it consists of a process of self-determination of his subjectivity through which I can say that I am a personal being.

Wojtyla, then, evaluates man from both the metaphysical point of view as a personal subject and from the phenomenological perspective of human experience. Agreeing that "phenomenological experience captures the experience of the human person in all his contents," Wojtyla accepts the phenomenological method insofar as it "enables us to uncover this specific correctness of the experience which stems from it, exactly because it is directed toward moral values."[40] Keeping in mind the usefulness of the phenomenological method in the description of human experience, especially in the realm of ethical values, Wojtyla turns to metaphysics in order to find "the objective principle" and foundation of human nature. In conclusion Wojtyla writes:

> The last step which we can take in by the phenomenological method in the area of ethical investigations, immersing ourself, so

---

[39] *Osoba i czyn*, p. 17.
[40] *Ocena mozliwosci zbudowania etyki chrzescijanskiej w oparciu o system Maksa Schelera* (Lublin: Towarzystwo Naukowe KUL), 1959, p. 123.

to speak, in ethical experience as in the specific ethical value which is unveiled in it, is this ethical correctness. Through this method we uncover good and evil; we see how it fashions the experience of a person. We cannot, however, delineate the objective principle through which we would be able to establish that one act of a person is ethically good, and another ethically evil. In order to formulate this principle we have to discard the phenomenological method. This particular moment of the problematics, which forces us to pass over in ethical inquiries from the phenomenological method to the metaphysical one, remains still in the realm of phenomenological experience, since we are phenomenologically asserting the normative character of ethical values in the analysis of the act of conscience; which by itself, as an experience, remains still in the field of phenomenological experience. The normative activity of conscience forces us to search for the objective reasons, that is, the measures of moral good and evil of our act. We have to avail ourselves here of the metaphysical method which will enable us to define the Christian, revealed order of moral good and evil in the light of an objective principle; it will enable us to define and justify it in a philosophical and theological manner.[41]

---

[41] *Ibid.*, p. 124.

VIII. HUMANISTIC PERSONALISM

In the case of any genuine philosopher it is sometimes very difficult to determine exactly the *novum* of his philosophy, and to evaluate justly the significance of his philosophical vision and its usefulness to the practical life of man. This is particularly true in regard to the philosophical anthropology of Karol Wojtyla. In the year after its publication, *Osoba i Czyn*[1] (*Person and Act*), his *magnus opus* evoked among the Christian philosophers in Poland a serious controversy, especially in regard to the method applied to his philosophy of man.

On December 16, 1970 a special symposium was organized at the Catholic University of Lublin, dedicated explicitly to Cardinal Wojtyla's book *Person and Act*. The participants described the methodology of *Osoba i Czyn* as based on both the

---

[1] (Kraków: *Polskie Towarzystwo Teologiczne*, 1969), p. 328.

classical theory of Aristotelico-Thomistic metaphysics with its terminology, and on the contemporary methods typical of phenomenology, hermeneutics and even linguistics. With an exclusion of the last, which he vehemently rejected, the author admits that in his "study there is plurality of languages and aspects (which) in the opinion of the author of *Osoba i Czyn* and many of the participants in the discussion indicates that there is basically duality", and as such the book "admits the analogy of the metaphysical terms in their fullness, e.g., *actus*, and *actus-potentia*. The author of *Osoba i Czyn* realizes that in his study he also brings about some sort of translation from one philosophical language to another."[2]

In view of the duality or even plurality of philosophical languages used in Wojtyla's philosophical anthropology, the question may arise as to what extent the author of *Osoba i Czyn* could avoid methodological syncretism. Not being myself an expert in philosophical methodology, and not having time to undertake a textual study of Wojtyla's book *Osoba i Czyn* in this respect, I will concentrate on the content of his interpretation of "Thomistic Personalism" (to use the title of one of Wojtyla's early articles in *Znak*), or "Humanistic Personalism" (to use the expression which Wojtyla applies to Thomistic anthropology as such) and to trace the philosophical implications of the Christian humanism.

I

For Max Scheler—as for any genuine phenomenologist— the basic and must fundamental element in his phenomenology is intuition (*Anschauung*) through which we can grasp the pure essence of things. "*A priori* everything is in the given intuition which belongs to the pure what and essence-sphere, i.e., the

---

2   "Slowo Koncowe", *Analecta Cracoviensia*, V-VI (1973- 1974), p. 257.

primordial notion (*Inbegriff*) of such essence-determinations (*Soseinbestimmtheiten*) of objects (in absence of *modi* of existence) which as *Sosein* are indefinable and which, for this reason, are presupposed in every attempt to define them. Such essence are, therefore, only 'intuitive.'"[3] Scheler's understanding of intuition is very close to that of Hénri Bergson: "(By) intuition is meant the kind of intellectual sympathy by which one places within an object in order to coincide with what is unique in it and consequently inexpressible."[4]

For Scheler, intuition precedes an object which is given in our experience (*Erleben*), and this object is given to us as a pure act without its form, thus constituting a specific dialectic between object and act. But an object deprived of its form and known only by intuition as a pure act is known only to us in regard to its essence and not to its existence. Intuition, therefore, is immanent in nature and essential in character, i.e., our knowledge presupposes some sort of "an innate" cognition. In his own words: "*Keine Erkenntnis ohne vorhergehendes Kenntnis; keine Kenntnis ohne vorhergehendes Selbstdasein und Selbstgegebenheit von Sachen*" ("There is no cognition without foregoing cognizance; no cognizance without foregoing self-existence and self-giveness of things").[5]

The aim of intuition, then, is to give direction (*Einstellung*) towards the essence of an object as a given fact in experiencing it by our mind. In other words, our mind intuitis (*ershaut*) the essence of an object as a fact, given in our experience, without any mediation of judging, defining, or analyzing. Our cognition, therefore, must of necessity be relative; namely, that the real forms of observed and experienced things are not taken from the

---

[3] *Vom Ewigen im Menschen*, in *Gesammelte Werke*, Bd. 5 (Bern: Francke Verlag, 1954), p. 196f.

[4] *An Introduction to Metaphysics*, trans. by T.E. Hulme (London & New York, 1912), p. 7. On Scheler and Bergson, see: John Nota, *Max Scheler: The Man and His Works* (Chicago: Franciscan Herald Press, 1983), p. 15, passim.

[5] *Schriften aus dem Nachlass*, in *Gesammelte Werke*, Bd. 10, ed. 1957, p. 397.

forms of the concrete objects themselves, but are (by our intuition)--so to speak--carried within the acts of our mind.[6]

Things as such (*die Sache selbst*), then, cannot be observed in their existing forms, nor can the intuited forms carried by the acts of our minds be either proven or disproven. Consequently, all human knowledge and philosophy is the result of *a priori* cognition and the pure essences are manifest and brought to exhibition (*zur er-schauung bringen*) to the human mind by our immediate and immanent intuition. In the words of Scheler: "Philosophy, in its nature, is strictly evident and for all fortuitous being a priori valid insight, neither increasable nor destructible by induction, into all essences and essential connections (*Wesenszusammenhange*) of being available to us in examples, that is, in both the order and realm of levels in which they are in their relation to its essence."[7]

In approaching Karol Wojtyla's philosophy, the reader will, at first, find many affinities between the thought of the Cardinal from Kraków, and the phenomenology of Max Scheler. Wojtyla uses terms which are familiar to the phenomenologists, e.g., "phenomenological criterion," "phenomenological inspection," "phenomenological wholeness," "phenomenological method," and especially "phenomenological experience." For the Archbishop of Kraków, phenomenology "facilitates an analysis of ethical facts on the phenomenal and experiential plane."[8] "Phenomenological experience captivates the experience of the human person in all its contents."[9] "Phenomenological method enables us to uncover this specific correctness of the experience which

---

[6] Cf. Manfred S. Frings, *Max Scheler* (Pittsburgh: Duquesne Press, 1965), p. 178f.

[7] *Vom Ewigen* in *Menschen*, p. 98.

[8] *Ocena mozliwosci zbudowania etyki chrzescijanskiej przy zalozeniach systemu Maksa Schelera* (Lublin: Towarzystwo Naukowe KUL, 1959), p. 122.

[9] *Ibid.*, p. 123.

stems from it, exactly because it is directed towards moral values."[10]

Wojtyla repeatedly stresses that his philosophy can be called phenomenological, and he points specifically to the influence which Max Scheler exerted upon his philosophical thoughts in the following areas:

1. Phenomenological experience as the basis for understanding man as a person through his acts: "Max Scheler helped me to discover that specific experience, which lies at the basis of the concept 'actus humanus.'"[11]

2. The phenomenological concept of human act: "for the act is the fullest manifestation of man/person in the dynamism proper only to him."[12]

3. Phenomenological identification and "the absolute connection between the experiences of man and the experience of morality."[13]

4. Phenomenological description as it helps to build a proper philosophical anthropology: "...for the propagation of only anthropology, for the building up of a philosophical image of man/person, we shall be compelled in a sense to place outside its scope the very study of moral values...still, the *de facto* reality of those values and the experience of them will constantly be present in our work."[14]

While accepting some phenomenological insights in his axiology, Wojtyla reproaches the philosopher from Jena for lacking "the objective principle" according to which "one act of person could be ethically good and the other one ethically

---

[10] *Ibid.* 4
[11] "The Intentional Act and the Human Act that is, Act and Experience,' *Analecta Huserliana*, 5 (1976), p. 278.
[12] *Ibid.*
[13] *Ibid.*, p. 279.
[14] *Ibid.*

evil."[15] Moreover, phenomenological intentionality is unable to objectively explain human act:

> When we say that self-determination given in the total human experience leads us in our analysis towards the acts of the will, then at the same time we have to recognize the insufficiency of any analysis, which represents this reality in the phenomenological terms of an intentional act.[16]

For this and many other similar reasons, Wojtyla comes to the conclusion that he has "to pass over in ethical inquiries from the phenomenological method to the metaphysical one."[17] The basic failure of Scheler is-- according to Wojtyla-- the wrong understanding of phenomenological intuition and the lack of a proper interpretation of human experience. As a result of these inadequacies, "we have to discard the phenomenological method," because "the normative activity of conscience forces to search for the objective reasons, that is, the measures of moral good and evil of our acts."[18]

Although Wojtyla himself uses a phenomenological term "inspection", his *oglad* is not the same as Scheler's *Anschauung*. For Wojtyla, *oglad* has metaphysical meaning, and for Scheler *Anschauung* is rather ontical in its function.[19][20] *Oglad* is a self-manifestation of man through which he reveals himself as subject of all his actions. When we say "man-acts," what is revealed is not only pure action, but man as subject as well. This is manifest by the intellectual act of inspection: "action is a specific moment of inspection grounded on the fact that man acts

---

[15] *Ocena mozliwosci*, p. 124.
[16] "The Structure of Self-Determination as the Core of the Theory of the Person," in *Congresso Internazionale Tomasso D'Aquino nel suo Settimo Centenario* (Rome/Naples, 1974), p. 40.
[17] *Ocena mozliwosci*, p. 124.
[18] *Ibid*.
[19] Cf. M. S. Frings, p. 188.
[20] *Osoba i czyn*, p. 14.

in his innumerable repetitiveness."[21] This repetitiveness of actions is also the best test to realize the fact of manifestation as "man-being-in-the-world." Wojtyla asks:

> What is, in this case, the meaning of 'manifestness?' First of all, in its cognizance, it seems to point to the essential characteristics of revealing and visualizing the object. 'Manifestness' denotes at the same time, that the understanding of the fact, 'a person acts;' is an act of a person, or better yet, is a totality of 'person act', and finds its full proof in the content of experience, i.e., in the content of the fact 'person' acts in the immense repetitiveness.[22]

The "countless repetitions" of man's actions point, however, not only to one self-manifestation in reality. It is also the foundation for experiencing him as person. While the experience of man as a person is a predominant idea in Scheler's philosophy, Scheler nevertheless neglects the objectivity of the existence of the real concrete person in his phenomenological intuition. Scheler can only intuit the essence of what person is experiencing, but without apprehending his concrete objective reality. Wojtyla as an ethician finds in Scheler's description a lack of the objectivity of moral values, and accuses him of failing to explain properly the very nature of human experience, especially good and evil, obligation and responsibility.

Wojtyla asks: "Why has Scheler failed (to explain) the internal structure of a very simple act that man is the causative originator and author of good and evil acts, and for which man is either rewarded with feeling of merit or guilt."[23] In his interpretation of values Scheler fails to recognize that they are the products of human actions through which "man experiences himself as the cause of values."[24] Moreover, depriving man of being "the causative principle" of human values, Scheler

---

[21] *Ibid.*
[22] *Ibid.*
[23] *Wyklady Lubelskie* (Lublin: Towarzystwo Naukowe KUL, 1986), p. 34.
[24] *Ibid.*, p. 35.

denies also that man is the source of his experiences. In conclusion Wojtyla summarizes his critique of Scheler's phenomenology: "If Scheler does not see this fact (i.e., the causality of man's actions), then his concept of person is at stake, the concept of person that is emotionalistic. In view of this he puts into question the experience itself...."[25] In a word, for Wojtyla "the person is a causative source of his actions, and through them the acts are the cause of their ethic validity, either positive or negative."[26]

II

Given that person is the causative source of experiencing values, the question arises: what is the element that makes values objectively good or evil? In order to answer this question we must ask how Wojtyla views the metaphysical nature of human person. In other words, how can we define man as a person and his constitutive elements which make the author of his own actions. Referring to the well-known historical dispute on Trinity and the Christological question,[27] Wojtyla accepts as a working definition of person, that proposed by Boethius: *Individua substantia rationis naturae.*[28]

---

[25] *Ibid.,* p. 35f.
[26] *Ibid.,* p. 36.
[27] The first who applied the term 'person' to the Trinity was Tertulian: "Custodiatur oeconomiae sacramentum quae unitatem in Trinitatem disponit Patrem et Filium et Spiritum Sanctum," *Adv. Prax. Patrologia Latina,* 2, c. 18; "Quaecumque ergo substantia sermonis fuit, illam dico personam et illi nomen Filii vindico," *ibid.,* c. 186. On the identity of 'persona' and 'hipostasis', cf. *St. Gregory of Nyssa,* Oratio XXI, *Patrologia Graeca,* 35, c. 1124-1125; De communibus notionibus, PG, 45, c. 185. For the ethymology of the term 'persona', cf. Trendelenburg, "Zur Geschichte des Wortes", *Kant Studien* (1908).
[28] De dualis naturis et una persona Christi, *Patrologia Latina,* 64, c. 1373.

In the medieval ages, Boethius's definition of person remained unchallenged. It was commonly accepted not only in theology but in philosophical anthropology as well. In this respect, Etienne Gilson observes: "there were practically no philosophers in medieval times who would not accept Boethius's definition as a sufficient one, because it satisfied the accepted view on (human) reality."[29] Medieval thinkers were only trying to clarify and qualify what kind of characteristics could be derived from Boethius's description of person as an individual substance of rational nature. The most frequent characteristics applied to human person were "incommunicabilitas", "*individualitas*", "*dominum sui actu*", "*sui juris*," etc. Although St. Thomas uses all the above characteristics, the most frequent and preferred qualities Aquinas attributed to human person are: *subsistentia* and *suppositum*, which we often find in Wojtyla as well.[30]

In modern times, however, philosophers gradually abandoned the notion of person as an insufficient principle to explain human nature. Beginning with Descartes, the very concept of substance was radically changed; for him 'substance' is no longer understood as *ens in se* or *ens per se*, but as "a thing which exists in such a way, as to stand in need of nothing beyond itself in order to its own existence."[31] Such an absolutistic understanding of substance led Descartes to the conclusion that created substances cannot be known in their existence, but only in their attributes.[32] Since in man the principal attribute is thinking, man should be understood as *res cogitans*, and person is only an expression for and manifestation of self-consciousness.

---

[29] *L'Esprit de la Philosophie Medievale* (Paris: J. Vrin, 1944), p. 207. Cf. H. Marshall, "Boethius definition of persona and mediaeval understanding of the man theater," *Speculum*, 25 (1950), pp. 471-482.

[30] Cf. *Osoba i czyn*, pp. 94ff.

[31] "Principia Philosophiae", I, 51 , in : *Oeuvres de Descartes*, VIII (Paris: L. Cerf, 1905), p. 24.

[32] *Ibid.*, I, 52; p. 24-25.

Following Descartes,[33] John Locke,[34] Gottfried W. Leibniz,[35] and Christian Wolff[36] stress self-consciousness as the principle attribute of person. But, since attributes follow being, man can be understood as person in various ways, depending on a particular philosophical anthropology. When David Hume, therefore, denied substance altogether, because we do not have any impression of it, then person became a meaningless notion. Losing the metaphysical ground and ontological foundation, person was reduced to moral and ethical spheres. In this respect, Immanuel Kant writes:

> Everything in creation, except one thing is subject to the power of man, and can be used by man as a means to an end, but man himself, man the rational creature, is an end in himself. He is the subject of moral law and is sacred by virtue of the autonomy of his individual freedom....Personality exhibits palpably before our bodily eyes the sublimity of our nature."[37]

The Kantian idea of person as an ultimate ethical norm makes man the principle of self-realization of his nature. But by the same token, Kant overstresses man's individuality by making him an autonomous being who is also the final foundation of all human values. In this way Kant becomes a father of many contemporary personalistic theories which--to use Gordon W. Allports' words "agree a) that the personality is of supreme value, b) that persons are to be distinguished metaphysically from things, and c) that subjective experience is the final psychological court of appeal."[38] Gradually person was

---

[33] For the adherents of Descartes, see: Ueberweg/Heinze, *Grundriss der Geschichte der Philosophie*, Bd. III (Basel-Stuttgart: Benno Schwabe & Co. Verlag, 1958), p. 244.

[34] *An Essay Concerning Human Understanding*, Book II, ch. XXVII, sec. 9.

[35] *Hauptschriften zur Grundlegung der Philosophie*, ed. by E. Cassirer, 1906, v. II, p. 184.

[36] *Psychologia rationalis*, sec. 741, p. 660.

[37] *Kritik der Praktischen Vernunft* (Reimer Verlag, 1908), p. 87.

[38] *Personality. A Psychological Interpretation* (New York: Henry Holt and Company), p. 33.

reduced to personality, and man as a person becomes just "a multiform dynamic unity."³⁹ Consequently, losing his subjectivity and becoming "the supreme value" (J.W. Goethe), man in his personality reaches a unity "not by the suppression of natural instincts, temperament, and capacities, but by permeation of them with a common spirit--the power of finding freedom, not <u>from</u> them, but <u>in</u> them."⁴⁰

Viewing man as the ultimate ethical norm and the sole "end in himself" is a self-defeating proposition, because man as a person ceases to be a subject of his own and is left to "the autonomy of his individual freedom." The first philosophers who realized the danger of all the implications of reducing person to personality were Max Scheler and Nicolai Hartmann. Both point out that the central conception of ethics is not the duty and obligation but the idea of person itself. But, in his understanding of person, contrary to Scheler's human subjectivity, Hartmann views man as a true bearer of both values and non-values.

For Hartmann, person as a subject is not only ontological entity, but is also an axiological one. But Hartmann understands values as essences arranged according to some hierarchy, namely, the higher value is subjectivized in the lower ones. However, person as a subject is only a determiner which values man ought to realize and which not according to the principle "the ought-to-be is in its nature an ought-to-be-real."⁴¹ But to answer what is the motive power to determine which values "ought-to-be-real", Hartmann recalls the Stoic teaching on *logos*, the neo-Platonic doctrine on *psyche tou pantos,* or even the Aristotelian concept of *nous*, which is supposed to be the ultimate principle of elevation of person and his values to be

---

39 William Stern, *Die Menschliche Personlichkeit* (Rodardr, 1919), p. 4.
40 H.S.W. Hetherington & J.H. Muirhead, *Social Purpose* (New York: Macmillan, 1918), p. 104.
41 *Ethics* (London: Allen & Unwin, 1932).

the divine.

Hartmann's system of ethics is onto-axiological without the metaphysical foundation which is needed to show the proper relation between person and values, namely, ontology and axiology. In order to establish the objectivity of ethical principles, it is not enough to examine the relationship which takes place between person and values, but it is imperative to establish first the metaphysical structures of person as an individual entity which is capable of existing independently. And only then can we examine the ontological functions of person, who--in his subjectivity--dispenses values through his actions. In a word, to view person metaphysically as a subsisting subject in the ontic realm of being, we must accept cause/effect relationship, and then to analyze person both in its metaphysical nature and its phenomenological functions.

Wojtyla could not find such a distinction between metaphysical nature and phenomenological function of person in either Scheler or Hartmann. Scheler's emotional experiences which are to establish interpersonal relationships cannot suffice to build an objective value system in ethics because they lack an individual will, which--according to Scheler--occurs only "on the margin (*auf dem Rücken*) of willing. A comprehensive study of experience shows that moral values are interiorly connected with that entire process of the will, which can rightly be called 'drama' because of its own proper dynamic structure."[42] Similar dynamic structures of person are also lost in Hartmann's doctrine on subsisting values which are of essential nature, because of their apriorism,[43] and lack of objective principle.[44]

---

[42] "The Intentional Act", p. 275.
[43] *Ibid.*, p. 274ff. Although Hartmann is not quoted directly by Wojtyla, his Ethics is enlisted in Wojtyla's Ocena mozliwosci as one of the basic source books.
[44] Cf. *Ocena mozliwosci*, p. 124.

III

In his metaphysical interpretation of person, however, Wojtyla following the Aristotelian tradition proposes to learn whether the ontic constitutive element of person can be found in rationality, as it is in Aristotle's definition of man as *zoon logistikon*. Wojtyla writes: "The usefulness of Aristotle's definition is unquestionable. It dominated metaphysical anthropology and fathered many different branches of science, which treated man as an 'animal' with the specific difference of rationality..."[45] However, Aristotle's definition of man is cosmological, because it reduces man to "an object, <u>one of the objects of the world,</u> to which visually and physically he belongs. <u>Objectivity,</u> thus conceived, <u>was connected</u> with the general principle, of the <u>reducibility of man.</u>"[46]

The reducibility of man to the objective world by defining him in the category of species and genus was an unavoidable fact for two reasons:

1. the impossibility of defining the individual existent (*to de ti*);

2. the hylomorphic structure of all natural things (including man) as proposed by Aristotle to be the most universal paradigm to explain the whole reality in its totality.

Wojtyla is aware of the necessity of using the principle of reducibility to explain nature and man scientifically:

> The whole scientific tradition of the complexity of human nature, of the spiritual and bodily *compositum humanum*, which through scholasticism passed from the Greek to Descartes, moves within the limits of this definition, that is, on the basis of the conviction as to the essential reducibility to the level of the world of that which is essentially human. It cannot be denied that enormous fields of

---

[45] "Subjectivity and the Irreducibility in Man", *Analecta Husserliana*, VII (1978), p. 108.
[46] *Ibid.*, p. 109.

experience and particular sciences, based on the principle of reducibility, follow this conviction and are working to ground it even more firmly.⁴⁷

The Cardinal from Kraków, however, also insists that there is a genuine feeling that man is definitely different from other things, and he cannot be totally reduced to the world of pure objects. Man is a subject which he is irreducible in nature and whom we call a person. First of all, "<u>we feel today a greater need than ever before</u>, and we also see <u>greater possibilities of the objectivization of the problem of man's subjectivity.</u>"⁴⁸ As a matter of fact, there is also an historical experience which indicates that there was a constant urge to view man as irreducible being in the world:

> <u>On the other hand,</u> it seems, however, that <u>the conviction of the primordial originality of the human being,</u> and hence of his <u>essential irreducibility to the level of the world</u> and of nature is as old as the need of reduction, expressed in Aristotle's definition.⁴⁹

The fact of irreducibility of man to the world and nature, the thinkers of all times sought in terms of person: "This conviction is at base of the understanding of man as a person, which has also a long history in the annals of philosophy, and today is at the foundation of the growing interpretation of a personal subjectivity of man."⁵⁰ As a matter of fact, accepting man as a subject which is irreducible to the world of natural things, it does not stand in contradiction to Aristotle's definition of man as *zoon logistikon*, because in its formulation it does not say whether man is an object or a subject: "We must admit that the manner of treating man as an object does not immediately result from Aristotle's definition itself; and especially that it does not belong to the metaphysical

---

47 *Ibid.*, p. 108f.
48 *Ibid.*, p. 107.
49 *Ibid.*, p. 109.
50 *Ibid.*

conception of man in his philosophical current."[51]

Wojtyla then, accepts both views on man: cosmological and personalistic in his metaphysics of man. The cosmological dimension of man reduces him to the world of objects, because man by <u>having</u> body necessarily belongs to the order of natural things. The personalistic dimension of man cannot reduce him entirely to pure objects, because by being a subject, man transcends the limits of the order of natural things. Discussing the proper understanding of progress, John Paul II, says:

> What is in question is the advancement of persons, not just the multiplying of things that people can use. It is a matter--as a contemporary philosopher (Gabriel Marcel) has said, and as the Council has stated--not so much of 'having more' as of 'being more.'[52]

How to overcome this apparent dichotomy between viewing man as an object immanent in the world of natural things, and man as a subject absolutely transcendent of any object of this world? In resolving this dichotomy between cosmological and personalistic views on man, we must distinguish between the horizontal and the vertical order of man in nature. In the horizontal order man exists in this world as an object, among other objects of natural things by the fact of <u>having</u> a body, and his subject-person is an ontological diversified unity determined by space and time; in this order man can be viewed in terms of substantiality and he is explained according to the Aristotelian hylomorphism. In the vertical order he is viewed as transcending being of the world of object and is seen as a subject by <u>being</u> person who can experience his irreducibility to natural things by using them as means for self-experiencing, and by developing his spirituality. In this order man is evaluated as a subsisting individual being of his own.

---

[51] *Ibid.*

IV

The re-formulation of Aquinas's conception of man into a 'person-act' enables Wojtyla to juxtapose the philosophical Christian humanism to the individualistic and collectivistic vision of human nature. Wojtyla opposes both Sartre's view of man as a pure 'self-consciousness' by stressing the ontological moment of 'self-possession' of each individual person, and Marx's view of man as a 'species-being' by distinguishing in man's *praxis* between the transitive and non-transitive aspects of human acts: "We maintain the principle of personalism against that of individualism and of totalitarianism. Both these conceptions destroy in the human person the possibility and even the ability of participation. They deprive man of his right to participation."[53]

Christian humanism as viewed by Wojtyla is not as yet realized, but it is rather a task to be achieved. It seems to the author of this essay that this was the main objective of the first encyclical of the new pontiff, "Redemptor Hominis." Quoting St. Augustine, "You made us for yourself, Lord, and our heart is restless until it rests in You," our new Pope comments: "In this creative restlessness beats and pulsates what is most deeply human--the search for truth, the insatiable need for the good, hunger for freedom, nostalgia for the beautiful, and the voice of conscience" (IV, 18).

---

[53] "Participation or Alienation" (from unpublished manuscript, p. 17).

www.ingramcontent.com/pod-product-compliance
Lightning Source LLC
Chambersburg PA
CBHW071454150426
43191CB00008B/1340